D1492418

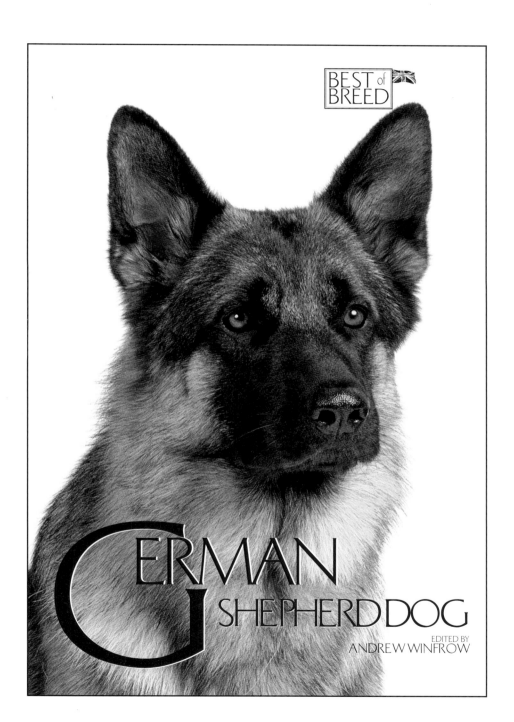

BEST of
BREED

GERMAN
SHEPHERD DOG

EDITED BY
ANDREW WINFROW

ACKNOWLEDGEMENTS

The publishers would like to acknowledge the following for help with photography: Metropolitan Police Dog Training Establishment, Guide Dogs for the Blind Association, Hearing Dogs for Deaf People, Pets As Therapy, Nikki Farley (Nikonis); John and Gill Ward (Belezra); Katrina Stevens (Kesyra); and Lucy Koster (Harana).

Cover photo: © Tracy Morgan Animal Photography (www.animalphotographer.co.uk)
page 2 © istockphoto.com/photopix; page 10 © istockphoto.com/Claudia Steininger
page 16 © istockphoto.com/Jan Tyler; page 41 © istockphoto.com/Emmanuelle Bonzami

The British Breed Standard reproduced in Chapter 7 is the copyright of the Kennel Club and published with the club's kind permission. Extracts from the American Breed Standard are reproduced by kind permission of the American Kennel Club.

THE QUESTION OF GENDER
**The 'he' pronoun is used throughout this book instead of the rather impersonal 'it',
but no gender bias is intended.**

First published in 2008 by The Pet Book Publishing Company Limited
PO Box 8, Lydney, Gloucestershire GL15 6YD

This edition published 2010 by The Pet Book Publishing Company Limited

© 2008 and 2010 Pet Book Publishing Company Limited.

All rights reserved
No part of this book may be reproduced or transmitted in any form or by any
means, electronic or mechanical, including photocopying, recording, or by any information
storage and retrieval system,without permission in writing from the publisher.

ISBN
978-1-906305-32-1
1-906305-32-3

· Printed and bound in Singapore.

CONTENTS

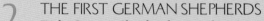

GETTING TO KNOW GERMAN SHEPHERD DOGS

Chapter

1

The German Shepherd Dog is one of the most popular breeds throughout the world, and it is not hard to discover why this is. The German Shepherd is a versatile, trainable dog that is highly regarded for his intelligence, loyalty, stamina and noble good looks. The Shepherd is the breed of choice for the police and military forces worldwide, and is also used as a guide dog for the blind and as an assistance dog. He is successful in competitive obedience, agility, working trials and other dog sports, and as a family companion his devotion and loyalty is second to none.

WHAT DOES A SHEPHERD LOOK LIKE?

The German Shepherd Dog is a working dog, ideally of medium height and size, strong, well muscled and alert. Slightly longer than its height, the male is larger than the female. The ideal height for the adult male is 62.5 cm (25 in) and 57.5 cm (23 in) for the adult female. A deviation of 2.5 cm (1 inch) above or below these measurements is acceptable.

Overall, the relationship between the height to length, and the placement and position of the limbs (angulations) should be such as to enable a far-reaching and enduring gait. The ideal weight of the male should be 30 kg to 40 kg (66-88 lb), and the female 22 kg to 32 kg (48.5-70.5 lb) – all relative to the height and strength of the individual. A Shepherd should give the appearance of strength

MEASURE FOR MEASURE

A German Shepherd is measured by depressing the hair at the withers – the highest point of the body, immediately behind the neck – and taking a straight line, touching the elbow (from behind) to the ground. Any increase above or below these maximum and minimum heights is faulty and must be regarded as detracting from the breeding value and working ability of the dog.

The German Shepherd Dog is a strong, well-muscled dog, and is slightly longer than his height.

comparative to his size, and the masculinity of the males and femininity of the females should be well defined.

HEAD BREED
The German Shepherd's head should be proportionate to the body without being coarse, too fine or over long in the muzzle. The general appearance should be slightly broad between the ears. The forehead should be very slightly domed with little, or, at the most, only a slight trace of centre furrow when viewed from the front or side. The top of the head

(approximately 50 per cent of the whole length of the head) should, when viewed from above, taper gradually from the ears to the tip of the nose without too pronounced a stop and running into a wedged-shaped strong muzzle.

Both the top and bottom jaws should be strong and well developed, with the bottom jaw clearly visible when the mouth is closed. The width of skull should correspond equally with the length: in the case of males, the width can be slightly greater and in females slightly less.

The muzzle should be strong

with tight lips. The bridge of the nose should be straight and should run evenly in line with the forehead.

COAT AND COLOURS
The weatherproof coat has a thick undercoat; the outer coat consists of straight, close-lying dense hair, which is longer and thicker around the hindquarters and neck. This is the coat that is described in the Breed Standard. However, Shepherds can also be long-coated; it is estimated that around 10 per cent of Shepherds are born with a long coat. The hair

Long-coated Shepherds are popular with pet owners, but they cannot be exhibited in the show ring.

is considerably longer and does not lie close and flat to the body; therefore, this type of coat is not so weather-resistant and not accepted within the Breed Standard. Long coats are often popular with pet owners, as the length of coat has no effect on the Shepherd's temperament and trainability, but they do require very regular grooming to avoid the profuse coat becoming matted.

The Shepherd may be black with tan, gold or light-grey markings. Dogs of this colour have a solid black saddle, or a black saddle with grey interspersed. Other acceptable colours are: all black; all grey with lighter or dark brown markings, referred to as sables; and bi-colours, which are almost completely black but with some tan on the legs. The nose, in all colours, should be black. Dogs that lack good colouration of the mask, with yellow or light, piercing eyes, light nails or weak colours are pigmentation failings and are not desired.

White German Shepherds do crop up in litters from time to time. White German Shepherds cannot be shown, as the Breed Standard states that blue, liver or white colours are highly undesirable, and they are disqualified from competition in conformation classes throughout the world. The reason why white Shepherds are undesirable goes back to the original function of the breed: white-coloured dogs are too conspicuous to work as guards, and are not as effective as herding dogs – particularly when working over snow-covered terrain. White German Shepherds have their fans, and there are several specialist organisations that hold classes for the White German Shepherds.

GERMAN SHEPHERD COLOURS

Black and gold: The solid black saddle is contrasted with rich gold markings.

Sable: This colour has lighter or dark brown markings.

White Shepherds cannot be shown, but they have an enthusiastic following.

Black: This colour is correct, but not commonly seen.

SUMMING UP

The general overall impression given to the observer is that of a natural presence, strength, intelligence and suppleness, with everything in proportion. The impression conveyed in the Shepherd's movement, coupled with his physical and mental qualities, show the endurance required in a working dog that must be both active and alert.

THE SHEPHERD TEMPERAMENT

The German Shepherd has a lively temperament, but he must be obedient and adaptable. He must display courage and resilience in the defence of his owner and possessions. He should be observant, obedient, and a good housedog, friendly with the family, with children and with other dogs, and at ease with people in general. The overall impression should be of nobility, alertness and self-assuredness.

Analysing temperament is a complex subject, as it is a combination of inherited genetic endowment, the life experiences of upbringing, and how an individual dog was taught to behave. Each dog is unique, but the ideal German Shepherd is a calm, confident, loyal dog. He is highly intelligent, very active, courageous and inherently protective. He should never be nervous or shy.

German Shepherds are slow to mature and maintain their puppy playfulness usually until at least two years old. A Shepherd can be wilful and quite vocal, barking at

Can you provide a suitable home for a German Shepherd?

all sorts of things, and if a dog is not socialised and trained from an early age, he can take over the household.

THE RIGHT DOG IN THE RIGHT HOME

As a potential German Shepherd owner, you will need to give careful thought to the breed's general characteristics in relation to the home you can offer. Making the decision to own a German Shepherd just because you like the appearance of this striking-looking breed or you think they are born ready trained can have a disappointing outcome for you and the dog.

As far as a German Shepherd is concerned, an ideal home means being an integral part of a family and joining in with family activities. A Shepherd will find great joy in being given jobs to do and will enthusiastically fetch his lead or find your slippers. In order for a pet Shepherd to blend harmoniously into the family unit, he must be treated

As long as a sense of mutual respect is established, the German Shepherd will get on well with children.

consistently and fairly by all the members of the household.

The German Shepherd can be so devoted to his family that he can become over-attached to the exclusion of all outside of it, so it is important that he meets and mixes with visitors to the home and other people when he is out for a walk.

The German Shepherd is very adaptable and can live happily in many different types of home. However, there are certain important elements to any home that will help ensure that the German Shepherd will live up to his rightful reputation as a faithful and trustworthy family companion that is a pleasure to own, and a credit to you and the breed.

I have based my impressions of the ideal home on observations I have made during many years

instructing at a German Shepherd training club consisting mainly of owners with their family pets, and also advising on behavioural problems that probably could have been avoided if more consideration had been given to the suitability of the home environment.

German Shepherds are born with characteristics common to the breed, but each dog is an individual, and, even within a litter of puppies, each will have its own unique genetically inherited traits. An ideal home is where care has been taken to match the German Shepherd's personality to suit a particular family and lifestyle. Because of their size and high activity level, German Shepherds are better suited to a country home with access to suitable places for exercise. The garden needs to be

securely fenced, to keep them in and other dogs out, preferably big enough that, on an occasional day when it is not possible to take your dog out for a walk, an energetic game chasing a ball can be played to satisfy the abundance of energy.

German Shepherds can adapt to living in a town house with a smaller garden, but you must have significant time to provide adequate stimulation and a great deal of varied exercise outside of the small home confines; otherwise, boredom, frustration and usually destructive behaviour will result.

PET-FRIENDLY
Well known for his loyalty and devotion to his human family, a German Shepherd will often extend his loyalty to other dogs and pets in the family, living in

LIVING WITH CHILDREN

German Shepherds are good with children, but they must be taught to have mutual respect for each other. Children can be excitable and inconsistent, playing too roughly and over-stimulating the dog. This can result in nipping if the games get out of hand. It is important that babies and young children are not left alone with a Shepherd, as they may unwittingly do something to upset or hurt the dog. However, if a Shepherd is socialised correctly with sensible children, he will show an amazing gentleness with them and will form a lasting, trusting bond – one of the most endearing relationships.

A well-socialised German Shepherd is surprisingly tolerant of small animals.

harmony with other animals if he is raised with them. Careful introductions need to be made initially so that pets such as rabbits, guinea pigs, birds and cats are not viewed as prey animals.

Dogs in the same household can bond very strongly to each other, sometimes wanting each other's company more than they want their owners. This is a very natural form of loyalty from a German Shepherd to his own kind. Spending time training and playing with the dogs individually will help to ensure the owner remains in control.

TRAINABILITY

The German Shepherd has a high level of endurance, plus sensitivity to movement, sound and scent. He was originally bred as a herding dog, working flocks of hundreds of sheep on open pastureland. He would patrol all day long, and also protect the sheep from predators, working closely with the shepherd, ready to obey any instruction.

These inherited qualities make the Shepherd easy to train and are the reason why he is an excellent performer in many different activities. He is capable of learning quickly and this, coupled with the willingness to interact with his owner, makes training enjoyable and fun. Training will always be more successful if the owner takes the time to establish a good relationship with the dog, reflecting trust, confidence and companionship.

Most German Shepherds live very different lives compared to

This is a breed that needs regular, free-running exercise.

their working ancestors, but the ingrained inherited behaviour traits are still very strong. If these instincts are not given an outlet, some Shepherds may become over-excitable and very reactive in everyday situations. A Shepherd that retains his herding instincts may want to round things up – usually the family when out for a walk together – as he likes everyone to be in one place. A Shepherd can also be highly motivated by movement and can

be tempted to indulge in chasing moving objects, which can include joggers, cyclists, cars, other dogs. It is therefore important to channel the dog's chase instinct into a controllable game with a ball or other toy.

German Shepherds enjoy human contact and have a remarkable ability to communicate their emotions and intentions through their expressive facial movements and body language. The movement

and position of the tail and ears is a very clear indicator of how a Shepherd is feeling. An enjoyable part of owning such a breed is being able to interpret and understand your dog's state of mind and what he might do next.

EXERCISE
The adult German Shepherd loves and needs physical exercise. Being such an active, alert breed, exercise is essential for his mental and physical wellbeing. The type

A German Shepherd Dog thrives on having an outlet for his mental and physical energy.

of exercise is important, as it should be varied and fun. Just being taken for a walk along the same route around the streets on a lead, stopping at the same places while the owner has a chat with a friend, is not very stimulating; neither is being left out alone in the garden. German Shepherds have a curious nature and love the chance to explore new areas, such as woodland, open grassland and beaches. Varied exercises include plenty of opportunity to chase a ball or a toy and lots of free-running in safe surroundings, whatever the weather.

The amount of exercise depends on the dog's age and fitness. Growing puppies should not have too much strenuous exercise, as it can damage their developing joints and bones. A fully mature German Shepherd will enjoy as much exercise as the owner can give.

Although German Shepherds need exercise, in terms of an ideal home, plenty of room for the dog is not necessarily the most important feature. Their ancestral heritage means they need company, and, without a doubt, from a dog's point of view an ideal home means lots of quality time spent with his owner, enjoying each other's company.

STIMULATION

A German Shepherd is no couch potato and would struggle to

cope with the stress of an inactive life. He needs above-average commitment to socialising, training and exercising. There are so many activities that German Shepherds excel in, including leisure sports such as agility, heelwork to music, working trials, competitive obedience, and tracking. The mental and physical stimulation of these activities is a challenge that he will thoroughly enjoy.

The German Shepherd is full of fun and curiosity; he has a natural instinct to fetch and carry and is willing to retrieve all sorts of articles. If you hide your Shepherd's favourite toys around the house and garden, and then send him to find them, he will

The German Shepherd can be trained to sniff out drugs and explosives.

SUPREME SENSE OF SMELL

One of the German Shepherd's special skills is his scenting ability. The Shepherd brain has a very large olfactory lobe that can process amazing amounts of information from his sensitive nose. A Shepherd has 220 million sensory cells compared to a human's five million. As humans, we find it difficult to pick up on more than one scent at a time, as the strongest scent overrides all the others. We see the world through the primary sense of our eyes. A Shepherd experiences the world through his nose; his primary sense is smell.

A German Shepherd can distinguish and discriminate a faint or old scent against much stronger scents, ignoring all others if a particular scent has caught his attention, or if he has been trained to detect a certain odour.

have a chance to use his keen sense of smell to find different articles.

Whether you attend classes or teach basic obedience at home, training is a vital part of owning a German Shepherd. It you have a well-behaved dog, it not only makes your life easier, as you have a dog that you can take anywhere with confidence, but it also produces a happier, more contented dog, who will enjoy accompanying you to lots of different places.

Training your Shepherd and sharing an activity, such as one of the canine sporting disciplines, can be the most rewarding experience, building mutual trust and confidence. In the right home environment, this lively, intelligent, strong breed can be relaxed and calm inside the home with the family, but tremendously active when enjoying a game outside. In an ideal home the German Shepherd Dog and his owners will enhance and enrich each other's lives.

SPECIAL SKILLS
The breed has distinguished itself in its versatility to adapt both physically and emotionally to work in all sorts of demanding situations alongside mankind. No other breed is as effective in so many different types of work, because of the German Shepherd's agility, physical stamina, emotional drive, ability to learn very quickly and enjoyment in human companionship.

SNIFFER DOGS

The German Shepherd's acute sense of smell has been utilised in his role as a service dog, seeking out prohibited drugs smuggled through ports and airports. Dogs are trained to indicate the presence of drugs often under difficult conditions, such as busy and very noisy airports, or warehouses full of boxes and parcels. A trained sniffer dog can detect extremely low concentrations of many substances – even minute traces of drugs hidden in cars or wrapped in parcels.

Shepherds are used to seek out hidden weapons and explosives, and they have the incredible ability to detect land mines by sniffing out the explosives in the mines, therefore establishing which areas are safe and which are dangerous. These hidden landmines stay active long after the conflict in affected countries is over, so the job of clearing them is a dangerous one.

Training a German Shepherd as a mine detector is a long and painstaking process, as a mistake on the dog's part would cost lives. The dog has to be able to work in different sorts of terrain and identify the various types of explosives found in mines. When the dog locates the scent, he is trained to sit still to stay safe, and to alert his human partner, who marks the location so the mine can be removed. The dog and handler team may work together for six to eight years, and the bond of trust becomes very strong.

A trained Shepherd can follow the track of human scent, and this can be used in search and rescue and in police work, tracking down criminals.

SEARCH AND RESCUE

Another activity where the German Shepherd has proved very successful is search and rescue. His superior scenting ability, sharp hearing, endurance and weather-resistant coat enables him to cope with every extreme of weather conditions.

Search and rescue dogs are trained to find missing people by following scent that is carried on the air. They can search large areas very quickly, helping to find lost children, walkers and climbers. Often the areas are hard to reach and the dog and handler teams are deployed by helicopter and have to be winched into the search area. German Shepherds are also used to search for avalanche victims and people buried under demolished buildings after earthquakes or explosions. Working in atrocious weather or environment conditions, the Shepherd's physical and mental stamina and determination in seeking out human scent has saved many lives.

Because these victims can be buried deep beneath snow or rubble, a different style of search training has to be used, as the dog must sniff the ground for

POLICE DOGS

The German Shepherd is the preferred breed for police work worldwide.

Training begins when the Shepherd is a puppy.

The athletic German Shepherd can work in a variety of situations.

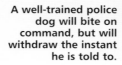

A well-trained police dog will bite on command, but will withdraw the instant he is told to.

scent rather than detect it from the air. Harnessing the German Shepherd's scenting skills and physical attributes has proved an invaluable source of help in a varied range of incidents involving life-saving activities.

POLICE DOGS

German Shepherds are very much an integral part of the police service and have proved to be the most suitable all-purpose breed. The Shepherd possesses the essential attributes to meet the varying circumstances in which police dogs are used, which include the following:

- Tracking to follow the trail of housebreakers or robbers
- Searching premises or open ground to locate suspects that have escaped or are hiding
- Searching for missing persons
- Recovering articles at crime scenes
- Assisting in crowd control
- General patrol and security patrol duties.

During criminal work, a police dog is required to chase and detain an escaping criminal, defending his handler or himself against attack. He may be required to disarm a criminal who has a weapon, and then guard and escort the criminal after detention.

ARMED SERVICES

German Shepherds working as search or patrol dogs for the armed services need to be highly confident, adaptable, and able to cope with foreign postings. The patrol work involves guarding military establishments, with skills similar to the police dog.

The Shepherd has to work well with his handler but be sufficiently adaptable to change allegiance when a handler moves on to other postings while the dogs stay at the original base. This highly specialist job suits the German Shepherd Dog.

ASSISTANCE DOGS

The German Shepherd's desire to please humans makes it the breed of choice for a variety of therapeutic occupations. Although other breeds, such as Labrador Retrievers and Golden Retrievers, are more commonly used as assistance dogs, the Shepherd is highly valued for his eagerness to work and his unparalleled devotion to his owner.

GUIDE DOGS

As early as 1919, German Shepherds were provided as guide dogs to lead war veterans who were blinded during the First World War. Today, guide dogs are used all over the world, and German Shepherds remain a popular choice. To be suitable as a guide dog, emphasis is placed on certain character traits of the German Shepherd, such as being calm and biddable, willing and responsive, confident and adaptable, and having above-average sociability.

After long and rigorous training, learning the skills needed to guide a visually impaired person, the dog and his new owner are introduced.

The German Shepherd Dog was the first breed to be trained as guide dogs, and they are still highly valued in this work today.

Matching a German Shepherd with his human partner is extremely important. The owner's height, length of stride, and lifestyle all play a part in making sure the correct partnership is formed. Once qualified and at home together, the guide dog can give his visually impaired owner the confidence to pursue an independent life.

SEIZURE ALERT DOGS

Over recent years a new kind of assistance dog has emerged. Seizure alert dogs warn people with epilepsy of an oncoming attack, allowing the person time to take seizure blocking medication, call for assistance, or get to a safe place where they

The German Shepherd's sound, trustworthy temperament makes him ideal for therapy work.

cannot hurt themselves. Seizure alert dogs have a natural ability to sense an oncoming attack, but quite how they detect the seizure is unknown. It is believed that the dogs sense or smell a change in the person's body chemistry or detect subtle changes in behaviour before a seizure occurs. The alerting behaviour is encouraged with food rewards.

A seizure alert dog must be trained with the person with epilepsy, as he needs to respond to that individual's specific pre-seizure activity. Alert dogs are trained to react to the impending seizure of the owner in various ways, including attention-getting behaviour, such as barking, whining, pawing and sometimes vocal or physical alert of other people. Trained dogs are able to give warnings as much as 10 to 15 minutes before the epileptic seizure occurs.

German Shepherds are very sensitive to their owner's moods and emotions, and are very quick learners, so they make an ideal choice for seizure response work. These dogs not only alert their owner but also are trained to fetch medicines, carry phones to their owner so they can summon help, and remain by their owner.

The German Shepherd is a multi-talented dog, but, perhaps most important of all, he is a companion *par excellence*.

A seizure can last from a few seconds to a few minutes and can cause unconsciousness; some sufferers fear having a seizure in public and avoid normal activities. The specially trained alert dogs can give their owners the courage and independence to live normal lives; the German Shepherd is their helper, protector, alarm system and companion.

THERAPY DOGS

The health benefit of animal companionship is now well documented, with studies proving that the affection and comfort that pets bring to people can relieve stress, lower blood pressure and raise spirits.

Therapy dogs are well-socialised pets, which are taken by their owners to visit nursing homes, retirement homes, convalescent homes, schools, special-needs schools, hospitals and many other establishments. In the UK, the organising charity is known as Pets As Therapy, and therapy dogs are referred to as PAT dogs.

Many German Shepherd pets have been registered as PAT dogs after passing a suitability assessment. The most important requirement is a sound temperament. A good therapy dog must be patient, friendly and gentle; he must enjoy human contact and be happy to be stroked and handled, even hugged, by unfamiliar people from children to the elderly. The therapy dog must not be concerned by sudden loud or strange noises, people with walking aids, or wheelchairs, and he must be at ease in all sorts of situations. Therapy dogs do not provide assistance, but some are taught to perform tricks during their visits, which adds to the enjoyment.

For animal lovers who are separated from their own pets or can no longer keep one, this service to the community by kind-hearted dog owners can bring much pleasure and have positive health benefits. A visit from a Pets As Therapy dog can even help people who are clinically depressed or children suffering from severe animal phobias. The benefits of this service are enormous.

SUMMARY

Getting to know the German Shepherd is to appreciate a superbly versatile dog that can live and work alongside us in many widely varying roles. His high energy and active mind can be misunderstood when not matched with the right owners, which could lead to this multi-talented breed of dog being unable to fulfil his true potential. From courageous protector, trusted assistance dog, to a devoted family companion, the German Shepherd has earned a special place in our hearts and our lives. I feel privileged to share so much of my life with this intelligent unique breed.

THE FIRST GERMAN SHEPHERD DOGS

Chapter 2

The story of the German Shepherd Dog began in 1891 when a small group of enthusiasts in Germany formed the Phylax Society. The aim of the group was to standardise the German herding breeds and to promote a native shepherd dog. Although the dogs shared the same role – herding and protecting livestock – they varied in size, shape and colour. In fact, the Phylax Society was short-lived, but was instrumental in setting a type for the German Shepherd Dog.

It was around 1894 that Captain Max von Stephanitz, who is known as the 'father of the breed', became involved. An enthusiastic supporter of the German Shepherd Dog, von Stephanitz was impressed by the breed's herding heritage combined with the intelligence, workability and strength of character. He established the Verein fur Schaferhunde – the SV – on 22 April 1899. This was the first breed club for the German Shepherd Dog and is now one of the largest breed clubs in the world.

EARLY GERMAN SHEPHERDS

The first dog to make a mark on the breed was Hektor Linksrhein, later known as Horand von Grafrath SZ 1 when he was renamed by von Stephanitz. He was born on 1 January 1895 and was bred by Herr Sparwasser. He was the first stud dog to be entered in the German stud records. If records are correct, he was a plain dog, who, if compared with today's Standards, would have resembled a crossbreed rather than a purebred animal.

In von Stephanitz's view, Horand was the ideal German Shepherd Dog. He described him as being: "Large... 60-61 cm, very good medium strength with powerful bones, beautiful lines and a nobly formed head; clean and sinewy in build." His character was also held in high esteem – "marvellous in his obedient faithfulness to his master". Von Stephanitz used Horand as the model for the first Breed Standard, which was drawn up in 1899. Von Stephanitz visualised a detailed Standard that would give a clear 'word picture' of the dog he wanted breeders to aim for. This Standard included the angles of bone, proportions and overall measurements, leaving little margin for individual interpretation. A system of records was put in place, and a breed register (Zuchtbuch) was set up, which included details of all existing German Shepherds and proof of their origin.

EARLY GERMAN SHEPHERD DOGS

Some of the Shepherds that played an influential role on the breed's early development.

Horand von Grafrath: The model for the first Breed Standard.

Hektor von Schwaben: A son of Horand and a Sieger in successive years.

Roland von Starkenburg: A grandson of Beowulf.

The first Sieger show was staged in 1899 and dogs competed for the coveted titles of Sieger and Siegerin – i.e. best male and best female in their class of Champions – as they still do today. The intention from the very beginning was a breed evaluation, focusing on construction, temperament and breeding. The first Sieger was a dog named Joerg von der Krone. His sire is not recorded and his dam was called Nelly. In 1900 and 1901 the continued influence of Horand von Grafrath was proved when his son, Hektor von Schwaben, was made Sieger in successive years. His dam was a working bitch, Mores Plieningen. Hektor sired the famous Beowulf out of Thekla von der Krone, who was a half-sister to Hektor. A Beowulf grandson, Roland von Starkenburg (Sieger 1906), had a major influence on future bloodlines. This came mostly through his son, the 1909 Sieger, Hettel Uckermark.

BREED SURVEYS

As the president of the Verein für Deutsche Schäferhunde (SV), von Stephanitz was very critical of the animals selected during the early development of the breed and some of those being used in breeding programmes. He was unhappy with the increased size, imperfect front angulation and general type. This was probably the result of using dogs of strong working ancestry.

For this reason von Stephanitz established the Breed Survey (Korung). The word 'Korung' comes from 'Kiesen', meaning 'to chose or select'. The first survey took place on 29 January 1922, and it gave an anatomical description, detailing the length, height, chest depth measurement, chest circumference, weight and general proportions. All these details were entered into the first Breed Survey book issued in 1922.

These records are still available today, and in Germany surveys still apply to all German Shepherds over the age of two years who wish to enter the breeding programme. Without working qualifications, no dog is allowed to breed. The book produced by the president, von Stephanitz, entitled *Der Deutsche Schaferhund in Wort and Bild – The German Shepherd in Word and Picture* – was to become the bible for the breed.

In 1925 Klodo von Boxberg was awarded the title Sieger. He was a medium-sized sable dog who produced the same type, but with better temperaments. He

Sieger 1925 Klodo von Boxberg: Sire of Utz.

Utz vom Haus Schutting, Sieger 1929: A return to the 'ideal' set out in the Breed Standard.

Sieger 1909 Hettel Uckermark SZ 3897: The Roland son whose correct size and harmonious build was recognisable in the descendants of Utz and Klodo.

also appears to have produced long coats. The tendency up till then had been towards a large, high animal, with a sharper temperament. Through his sons, Curt Herzog Hedan, Donar Zuchtgut and the 1929 Sieger, Utz vom Haus Schutting, came improvements in size, character, conformation and working ability – a return to the 'ideal' set out in the Breed Standard. Klodo was exported to the USA, where he had a major influence on the development of the breed.

Utz also proved to be a highly influential sire, and his bloodlines were instrumental in establishing the breed in the UK and in America. Interestingly, his bloodlines also saw a new colour – black and gold became established in the breed. But, yet again, temperaments weakened and there were also problems with missing teeth. Over the years that followed, with the introduction of Mutz von der Pelztierfarm (see Pillars of the Breed, page 29), came an improvement in temperament and working ability.

THE BREED SPREADS

A few German Shepherd Dogs were imported to the UK before the outbreak of the First World War, but the breed quickly declined in popularity as a result of anti-German feeling. The breed started to revive after the war when soldiers returned with tales of the heroic dogs that had been used to convey messages from the front line, to find the wounded, and who had served as loyal guards and companions.

One American soldier, Les Duncan, was so captivated with the breed that he brought a dog back with him. In 1918 he had found a German Shepherd puppy

in a trench on the Western front. He named the dog Rinty, and, when he was back in the USA, he trained him to become the legendary film star Rin Tin Tin. He was signed up by Warner Brothers Studios, and made 26 films before his death in August 1932. He received fan mail amounting to 10,000 letters a week. It was the heroic exploits of Rin Tin Tin that did much to promote the breed's popularity both in the USA and the UK.

In the early days, registrations recorded in the UK were relatively small. This was because the breed was championed by the upper classes, or by those who had experienced the breed in its country of origin. It took some time before the breed became more widespread. The situation in the USA was slightly different, and registrations were higher because the breed was also being used for its original purpose – herding and protecting livestock. This had an influence on breeding programmes, as dogs of influence were purchased and imported to the USA directly from Germany and were used to establish bloodlines.

Influential British breeders in those early days included: Lord Brabazon of Tara, Lt. Col Baldwin (Picardy), Mrs Gwen Barrington (Brittas), Lady Kitty Ritson (Tulchan), Mrs Howard (Seale), Mrs Iris Dummett (Charavinge), Mr and Mrs Brian Lindsay (Brinton), Nem and Percy Elliott (Vikkas), and many others.

THE VERSATILE SHEPHERD

In the early days of the breed, the SV approached the police authorities and suggested the German Shepherd Dog might be considered for patrol and protection duties. Von Stephanitz had always been keen to promote the breed's guarding abilities, which came from its original work, protecting livestock. Trials were conducted in 1903 and they were so successful that a police dog training and breeding centre was established near

CHANGE OF NAME

As a result of anti-German feeling, the word 'German' provoked controversy when the first German Shepherd Dogs first came to the UK. The breed was therefore renamed after the area from which it originated – Alsace Lorraine – which is on the German/French border. The German Shepherd Dog became known as the Alsatian Wolfdog. In the USA, the 'German' part of the name was also dropped, and the breed was known as the Shepherd Dog.

The term 'Wolfdog' did not do the breed any favours in Britain, and in 1924 this part of the name was abandoned and it was known simply as the Alsatian. In 1931, the American Kennel Club restored 'German' to the breed's name, but the UK was still reluctant to acknowledge the breed's origins. In 1936 a small concession was made and the breed was called the Alsatian (German Shepherd Dog).

It was not until 1977 that the German Shepherd Dog League of Great Britain approached the Kennel Club to request a change of name. The request was put to the vote, and the breed was renamed the German Shepherd Dog (Alsatian).

Berlin. During the First World War, the German Shepherd Dog was adopted by the armed forces and the breed's scenting ability was a major asset, combined with his work at sentry posts, giving warning of enemy approach.

The German Shepherd Dog was also used as the first guide dog, and, following this early success, Germany pioneered the

concept of the training of guide dogs for the blind. A training school was opened in Potsdam in 1923, and Britain followed suit, establishing its first training centre in 1931.

As the breed developed in the UK, its versatility was more fully appreciated and in addition to working as guide dogs, German Shepherds were trained for the Red Cross, the army, the RAF, the police, the prison service, for search and rescue, and for herding. Rin Tin Tin had proved that German Shepherds were ideal for film television work, and they were also highly valued in canine sports.

Within the police service, the German Shepherd became the breed of choice because of his all-round skills. The German Shepherd is agile, intelligent and fearless, capable of holding and stopping a person, with an excellent nose for tracking.

In those early days, the police were often given German Shepherds as gifts. In many cases, it would be because the dog had become too much for a family to cope with. As a result, many types were accepted, and there was no consistency of size or colour, just, in general, good temperaments. After breeding the occasional litter from these gift dogs without much success (and quite a few hereditary defects), the Metropolitan Police set up an excellent breeding programme, using stock from well-established kennels and healthier, modern-day bloodlines. Their dogs are now screened for inherited conditions, and German Shepherds working in police forces have become a credit to the breed.

At the same time that the breed was becoming increasingly valued as a working dog, it grew in popularity as a guardian and a loyal and trustworthy friend within the family environment, thus proving to be an excellent family companion.

WORKING STRENGTH

The first working trials event was held by the Alsatian League and Club in May 1927 under Kennel Club rules. The object of promoting working trials in the UK was to promote the practices of those in Germany who took into consideration the need for mental alertness as well as physical fitness as part of the Standard. Working trials is a test that allows the dog to develop his ability to do this through the five grades of qualifications. Both Schutzhund (which is the German equivalent) and working

TOP HONOURS

Crufts is the most prestigious dog show in the world, and it is the greatest honour to win Best in Show. There are three German Shepherds who have achieved this title:

- 1965: Ch. Fenton of Kentwood, owned and bred by Miss Sonica Godden.
- 1969: Ch. Hendrawen's Nibelung of Charavigne, owned by Mr and Mrs Edwin White
- 1971: Ch. Ramacon Swashbuckler, bred by Mr and Mrs Will Rankin and owned by Prince Ahmed Hussein.

trials in the UK are designed to achieve good control in obedience and tracking. In Schutzhund the third phase is protection.

Most dogs entered in the first working trials were imported, having received their training in Germany; they were also some of the best show dogs of their day. They included Danko de Versaillies, owned by Mrs Margaret Giffard, who was a great supporter of trials. Danko sired the three winning dogs: Crimstone Amigo, Aello and Bruna. In the open patrol dog trials, held in the second half of 1927, these three dogs took second, third and fourth place. The winner was an imported bitch: Ch. Armin Ernaslieb, owned by Mrs and Miss J.A. Workman of the Cesra kennel.

Many of the competitors were breed Champions who had obtained working qualifications. They included: Ch. Armin Ernaslieb also qualifying PH (a police dog qualification open to civilians in Germany), his son Ch. Adalo Ceara PD (a UK police dog qualification), and his litter sister Ch. Ansa Ceara, who also won the working trials certificate. The first working trials Champion was Asra v. Schurzfell.

In 1928, at the Association of Sheep, Police and Army Dog Societies (ASPADS) trials, Captain Max von Stephanitz graced the event and judged the trials.

DUAL-PURPOSE SHEPHERDS

Some breeders in the UK were aiming to breed a dual-purpose Shepherd, who could excel in the show ring, in workings trials, and in obedience, while others focused on producing dogs purely to exhibit in the show ring. The kennels that specialised in producing all-rounders were: Brittas, Druidswood, Romeno, Eveley, Sadira, Vikkas, Scripdean, and Letton to name but a few. Barbara Hill (Greyvalley), Charlie Wyant (Heelaway), and Bill and Heather Hardaway (nee Ricketts) also promoted the breed in obedience and working trials competitions. It was these dogs that became sought after by police and security services in the UK.

PILLARS OF THE BREED

It was not until the late 1960s that we saw four German dogs who were to have a great influence on the breed. They were:

- Mutz von der Pelztierfarm VA (Excellent Select) and Reserve Sieger: This dog was known for giving good temperament. He was lacking in pigmentation and his croup could have been better, but he was, nevertheless, a very good male.
- Canto von der Wienerau V (Excellent): A very good producer of good colour with a good croup, but somewhat lacking in character and cow-hocked in movement. Canto was, without a doubt, the leading sire of his day. Unfortunately, he was later implicated in the blood disorder of haemophilia.
- Quanto von der Wienerau VA (Excellent Select): An excellent quality male, with a very good masculine head and excellent angulation; his croup could have been longer and his pasterns firmer. As with Canto, he also sired a Sieger.
- Marko vom Cellerland VA (Excellent Select) Sieger: He was made Sieger in 1972 and was a popular stud and produced well. He was a good middle-sized male, with very good pigmentation, good proportions and a good croup. Marko was not favoured by many of the top kennels of this era, and therefore his line did not have the same impact as the other three males mentioned. It would appear that there was some criticism of the forequarters, and concerns over some sharpness in his character. In general he gave good croups, hips and shoulders, and some very good progeny.

These four dogs were hailed as 'pillars of the breed in the modern era', and they gave us the type of German Shepherd Dog we have today. Between them came many faults as well as good points, but in general they gave us a very definite type, which would influence the future of the dogs shown in Germany and around the world. Among the best known is Uran von Wildsteigerland, whose bloodlines have been used extensively, and is an acceptable type to all breeders worldwide.

THE INTERNATIONAL TYPE

In more recent times, we have seen the breed change to become more in line with Germany, and an international type has emerged. Some faults were introduced, although with careful breeding and a greater knowledge of bloodlines, the present-day breeders have eliminated the worst of these, and the breed looks to be in safe hands.

It was around the 1980s when there was a significant change in the breed. Many of the middle-of-the-road type of Shepherds, some long in proportions and deeper in the body, were bred to imported animals of totally different type. As time went on, we began to see a heavier German Shepherd with a thicker coat, particularly around the neck. In the late 1980s, a narrower and more stilted type emerged, who was shorter-coupled, with a more pronounced overline – commonly described as a roach back, where the middle of the back appears higher than the withers. Some imports could be blamed for these problems, but by using better imported dogs from some of the top show kennels (such as Bedwins and Vornlante) the breed began to resemble animals being shown in Europe and was praised by visiting judges from Germany.

The head became more defined with sex characteristics more pronounced, along with a slightly longer animal of the correct proportions: the length about 10-17 per cent more than the wither

Mutz von der Pelztierfarm.

Canto von der Wienerau.

Quanto von der Wienerau.

Marko vom Cellerland.

height. This is a range of 8.5:10 to 9:10 expressed in height to length. The very recognisable, far-reaching, floating trot, assisting a tireless and effortless movement when herding, was never lost. Temperament problems, which existed in the past, were vastly improved and we see less of the nervous, fear-biting dogs who were seen in some of the kennels that had a reputation for breeding dogs with weak temperaments. This improvement was undoubtedly due to importing some very good dogs, and breeders recognising the need to improve. When breeding, it is vital to ensure that both the sire and the dam have correct temperaments to produce puppies of the desired nature.

Missing teeth were a problem in this era; the eye colour began to change and, in some cases, started to become lighter than the Standard stated. Feet also caused some concern, as poor feet were often accompanied by weak pasterns.

Over the years, breeders have worked hard to eliminate these faults within the breed. The Breed Council Breed Survey, which now takes place throughout the UK, is run along the same lines as its German counterpart (without the protection phase). This enables us to evaluate the breed and keep up to date with its development and recommendations for breeding. The breed surveyors are Championship show judges who are elected by breed clubs and

Fina vom Badsee: Mother of Palme von Wildsteigerland.

Palme von Wildsteigerland.

Nick von der Weinerau: Sire of Palme von Wildsteigerland.

are then appointed by the GSD Breed Council.

Most British breeders have now moved forward and accepted the international type promoted by WUSV (World Union of German Shepherd Dog Clubs) throughout Europe and the rest of the world, who want the complete German Shepherd Dog and not just a show specimen.

MODERN BLOODLINES

A number of top sires and dams have had a major influence on modern bloodlines, and this has been cemented through careful line-breeding. A few faults did appear, such as the lack of forereach when trotting, and in some animals the sex was not instantly identifiable by looking at the dog's head and size alone.

But, overall, we saw a more balanced animal begin to develop, with no exaggeration, good colour, good type and correct mouths, as well as good movement.

Many of today's established kennels in Germany are world famous, including Wienerau, Wildsteigerland, Arminius, Arlett, Batu, and Farbenspiel. Dogs from these kennels can be seen in many pedigrees here in the UK. One top kennel that stands out is Wildsteigerland, owned by Martin Gobl, who served his apprenticeship over the years, studying and listening, watching and reasoning, and becoming very knowledgeable about the breed.

Martin purchased a young bitch called Fina vom Badsee,

who was mated to Nick von der Wienerau, a dog who had in his pedigree two of the original four previously mentioned sires: second-generation Canto von der Wienerau and third-generation Mutz von der Pelztierfarm. The mating produced the famous Palme von Wildsteigerland, who was born in 1979. She had a few litters and although she did not do well in the ring herself, she was a producer of fine animals. From her first litter to Irk von Arminius she produced the famous sire, Uran von Wildsteigerland. In 1982 Uran was shown with others from his litter, and was placed SG6 (Very Good). In 1983 he was entered in the working class and received VA8 (Excellent Select). He was seen by the Kormeister (the judge of males who assesses and grades dogs put before him) and was said to improve on type, general appearance and fitness. So when in 1984 he gained the title of Sieger VA1 at the tender age of three and a half years, it was not a surprise. The following year he was crowned again as Sieger VA1, and the judge remarked that his views had been confirmed, and that he had further improved from the year previous and he had become an outstanding sire.

The influence he had on the breed worldwide was highly significant; he had in his pedigree three of the famous four, Canto, Quanto, and Mutz. When taking his place at the head of his progeny group, followed by his offspring, it was an impressive sight that increased every time he appeared at the Sieger. The type became more imprinted with some truly excellent, highly graded individuals, many in top positions. This breeding has had an influence on today's German Shepherd breeding worldwide, proving he was the greatest sire in post-war years. His owner, breeder, and kennel will be recorded in history, as well as on so many of the modern-day pedigrees, through his descendants: Yambo vom Wildsteigerland, Palme von Bad-

Ch. Rosehurst Chris.

Boll, Uta v. Batu and other such notable dogs.

Herman Martin (Arminius Kennels) then acquired Palme and she was mated to Xaver von Arminius, producing the Sieger 1986-87 Quando von Arminius, another top producer, giving better heads than his half-brother Uran, and the pigmentation was also stronger. The likelihood was that top-quality males would come from Quando as opposed to Uran, and with the birth of Odin von Tannenmeise in 1984, this would come true, and was to have a great influence on the breed over the next 20 years.

The influence that a top German sire can have on the breed in other countries, and the value of good bloodlines, can be seen in Palme von Wildsteigerland and her sire, Nick von der Wienerau. Nick sired Ch. Cito vom Konigsbruch, a German import brought to England by Paul and Tracy Bradley of the Vornlante kennel. Cito probably had the greatest influence of any import in the past 25 years in the UK. He sired 17 Champions.

Uran, the son of Palme, was also the sire of another three top-class producers in the UK: Ch. Rosehurst Chris, Ch. Bedwins Pirol, and Ch. Exl vom Batu. This proves the value of the German system for promoting the best bloodlines to ensure the future of the breed.

THE SIEGER SHOW

The Sieger Show (Bundessieger Zuchtshau) is held in Germany every year around late August or early September. The whole event is a breed evaluation. This event is held over three days when the best German Shepherd Dogs in the world gather to compete for the coveted titles of Sieger and Siegerin, in the Youth, Young dog and Adult classes. The whole point of the Sieger Show is to see the progress made in the breed over the previous years due to the selection of the best dogs in construction, temperament and breeding. The judges are selected from the best in Germany and have a duty to promote the dogs that are correct to the Breed Standard and will benefit the breed for the future.

As well as the winners and grading for each individual in all of the six main breed classes, there are also progeny groups where the top sires have the opportunity to enter the ring followed by their offspring. This gives a chance to evaluate the vices and virtues from matings to many different females. It is from these groups that the eventual VA1 Sieger will be chosen from the males, and other good producers will be rewarded with a high position. The females are mainly judged on their previous show performance and breeding, and any offspring that have gained high positions at the

show. The adults shown all have to have Schutzhund titles and Korungs to be eligible to compete in the classes.

WORKING KENNELS IN GERMANY

Herding trials are organised in Germany each year, and it is wonderful to see the handlers, in traditional shepherd's uniform, working their dogs, showing off the skills they perform daily when at work. The German Shepherd is not only a herder but also a guarding animal, protecting the shepherd and the sheep from predators.

There are few kennels in Germany who are able to say they still work and show the German Shepherd. The Kirschental kennel breed to the Standard, but their dogs retain herding instincts. Eiko vom Kirschental was crowned Sieger in 1988, his sire was Uran, who

was Sieger in both 1984 and 1985. Two sons of Eiko became Champions in the UK. They were Ch. Moonwinds Golden Mahdi and Ch. Moonwinds Golden Emir, bred by Miss Pam Meaton.

In Germany there are also dogs that were bred purely to compete in the sport of Schutzhund. These Shepherds are often sable, black or bi-coloured, unlike those seen at conformation shows, who are mostly black and gold. They are selected for their working ability rather than their appearance, and their high energy is not always suitable for the first-time owner.

Schutzhund is a sport that involves a day-long test of the dog's character and trainability, evaluating his drive, willingness to work, and stability in three different phases, consisting of obedience, tracking and protection.

The tracking test assesses the dog's scenting ability and concentration. The obedience evaluates the dog's ability to work willingly and precisely, carrying out his handler's orders when heeling, retrieving, and jumping – plus a variety of other skills. In the protection phase, the dog's obedience and courage is assessed. This involves searching and warning his handler of a hidden person (villain), stopping an assault on the handler, and guarding and preventing the escape of the villain. Training for the sport of Schutzhund requires dedication

Eiko vom Kirschental; Sieger 1988.

and several years' commitment, with the handler and dog working as a team.

Only the dedicated person who is willing to train to a high standard and take the training very seriously could possibly cope with the type of dog used in the sport. This is a very mentally alert animal, and expert tuition for both the handler and the dog is needed in order to make this type of animal a credit to his owner and the breed. These dogs have been bred to think and obey with very quick reactions, and they are very impressive to watch when they are at work. Although dogs that compete in the conformation classes at the annual Sieger Show must have the Schutzhund qualifications, they are normally for the purpose of breeding and gaining the Korung (Breed Survey) and not for competing in trials on a regular basis.

THE GERMAN SHEPHERD IN AMERICA

The German Shepherd Dog continues to reign supreme as one of the most popular breeds worldwide due to its intelligence, good looks, loyal temperament, and versatility.

After the famous film star Rin Tin Tin had promoted an interest in the breed, the USA started to import selected stock directly from Germany in order to establish a correct type of animal. As highlighted earlier, one of the more famous dogs to be imported was Klodo von Boxberg, who went on to live in the

A fine example of an American German Shepherd Dog on the move.

Marelden kennels owned by Mr A. Gilbert. Klodo was imported to the USA to try to improve type. It was found that he produced better colouring because he was sable, and the temperament of his progeny was a little less sharp than they had been used to. Being a medium-sized dog, he started to produce animals more of the correct size, which saw the GSD becoming less prone to injury and more capable of working.

Other German dogs to follow were Pfeiffer von Bern, Zampano vom Oasis and Shalome vom Oasis. The American breeders were – and still are – keen to work their dogs and push them to their full potential. In certain

kennels, the type seen now has changed and often differs from the Standard set by the WUSV. In America there are those who choose to promote a different concept of the breed and like a slightly longer dog with more hind angulation, a longer upper arm, and a higher wither, because they claim that this produces a more efficient German Shepherd with a longer striding, more powerful gait. Even so, a large number of active breeders now follow the European and WUSV rules on breeding and performance, especially those who compete in the sport of Schutzhund.

Popularity of the German Shepherd Dog comes and goes,

Ch. Gayvilles Nilo: Breed record holder.

Ch. Nikonis Colin: This German Shepherd Dog is campaigned in Britain and in Germany with considerable success.

and demand may be greater in one year than the next; this increases if a German Shepherd wins Best of Show at a major event. Groups such as the monks of New Skeet in the USA promote the breed as a companion with excellent manners and trainability, and specialise in a working family companion. Originally, the monks were farmers working with livestock but when this became financially unfeasible in the 1970s they focused on producing and training sound and typical German Shepherds.

In Canada, the Royal Mounted Police has found the German Shepherd to be the ideal dog for its use. A special breeding programme has been set up, importing dogs with strong working ability from police forces in the UK.

THE CURRENT SCENE IN BRITAIN

So we are now recording the history of the present time, having gone through many phases, and remembered dogs like Uran von Wildsteigerland and Quando von Arminius in Germany and Ch. Cito vom Konigbruch here in the UK.

A new breed record holder has emerged from the top-producing Gayvilles kennel, an excellent male, Davy and Joan Hall's Ch. Gayvilles Nilo, sired by Ch. Rosehurst Chris, with an incredible 52 Challenge Certificates to his name. He is a grandson of the great Uran. Since Nilo's retirement, Dave and Sharon Bowen's (Lararth) German import Apollo vom Dakota, himself line bred to Uran and the Q-litter Arminius, sired Ch. Lararth Houdini, a quality male of excellent type and a consistent winner. To date, he has been awarded 16 Challenge Certificates.

The international type of dog has now become the norm, and after seeing many different types over the years – from long and low, to leggy and short-coupled – the future looks good. Details are on record of dogs that have suffered construction faults and

Ch. Lararth Houdini: A popular top winning male in the UK with 16 CCs.

health problems, and we now have breeders who are dedicated to improving the breed, strengthening character and type. They all have their place in the history of the German Shepherd Dog.

We also witness many groups who have decided to go their own way. Some prefer to live in the past, not wanting to move forward, with others wanting to buy success at the expense of gaining high awards without any consideration for the breed. Good breeding stock is not always from top show dogs, and changes cannot be implemented too quickly. It is important to remember that it has taken the breed over 100 years to get where we are today. Some breeders are being too influenced by what is happening in Germany and lose sight of the excellent dogs available in their own country. But this is progress and will be recorded in the breed's history to be read in later years by other enthusiasts.

The insistence by the WUSV that all member clubs follow the rules and record the parentage by DNA, as well as only breeding from correct types who are healthy and have been X-rayed for sound hips, means that the future looks good for the German Shepherd Dog. With more people following the principles of the WUSV we now have many UK exhibitors who have competed at the German Sieger, and have done the UK proud in their placings, making their mark in the breed.

It has also been reported that, in the near future, the Kennel Club will accept Schutzhund as a sport in the UK, which will be another major step to be recorded. So the influence of the breed in Germany has progressed and produced a very fine animal, which enthusiasts are proud to own and be associated with.

Long may the breed continue to prosper, proving it to be a noble breed worthy of any family home.

A GERMAN SHEPHERD FOR YOUR LIFESTYLE

Chapter 3

So you think you would like to own a German Shepherd Dog? Before making the decision to purchase a puppy, you will need to consider whether this highly intelligent, but often demanding breed is right for you and, indeed, whether you will be a suitable owner for him. This involves doing some extensive research about the breed before going to view a litter of puppies, as seeing a cuddly little bundle may prove hard to resist. Owning a German Shepherd is a long-term commitment, so it is better to know what you will be taking on before you buy. Many Shepherds end up in rescue centres because their owners had not given enough thought as to how much time and work a new puppy requires.

The German Shepherd requires a calm, assertive owner. If you are weak and unable to establish your authority, a Shepherd will rule the family. This sort of dog is at best a nuisance, and at worst a danger. On the other hand, if you are too harsh and inclined to bully, you will destroy your Shepherd's spirit and he will become withdrawn.

Taking on a new puppy is hard work and will alter your routine. You will need a great deal of time, patience and commitment. A puppy needs three or four feeds a day, and will need to be taken out into the garden at frequent intervals to assist with toilet training. A pup has little sense of right and wrong, so the ground rules also need to be established early on. Therefore a puppy requires a lot of attention, training and affection. Your lifestyle will change for the next 10 to 12 years, which is the average life span for a Shepherd.

THE PROS AND CONS

The German Shepherd is extremely intelligent, alert, loyal to his family and easy to train. He is versatile and biddable, making him popular with the police, and also obedience and working trials enthusiasts. He also loves agility, flyball and other competitive sports.

Being so intelligent, a Shepherd will learn bad habits just as quickly as good ones. Correct and consistent training is therefore very important, especially when he is growing up. It is no good waiting until your dog is older, as he will be bigger, stronger and may be set in his ways by then. The Shepherd is essentially a working dog, so he needs mental stimulation to keep his active mind occupied; otherwise he will be bored and may become destructive or excessively noisy, especially when left alone.

The Shepherd can become territorial, so it is extremely important that he is socialised frequently during the first year, so that he is a well-adjusted and sociable member of the family. Some Shepherds are not overly friendly to dogs with whom they are unfamiliar, so this is another aspect that needs to be dealt with. A puppy needs to be given the opportunity to play and interact with other dogs who are calm and good natured. Some Shepherds can be very noisy, dominant or strong minded, so will need the correct discipline, training and handling. Others are more sensitive and may need a more sympathetic and encouraging approach.

A German Shepherd will grow into a large dog very quickly, so he needs a good-sized garden and, when adult, will require plenty of exercise and daily walks, whatever the weather.

He will develop a double coat, which will need regular grooming, especially when he is moulting. During a moult, which can last around six weeks, he will leave clumps of hair on floors and carpets, or on anything he rubs up against, such as furniture or your best outfit! This will generally happen twice a year, although central heating may cause him to moult more often. If you are particularly house-proud, this aspect of owning a Shepherd will need to be considered. Neutering can also alter the coat texture, causing the coat to become 'woolly', making regular grooming essential. Long coats will also need extra grooming to prevent the coat getting matted or tangled; this type of coat tends to attract more mud and takes longer to dry.

FINANCIAL IMPLICATIONS

Apart from the obvious purchase price of the puppy, there are many other financial aspects to owning a Shepherd that need to be considered, many of which are ongoing expenses.

Firstly, there is all the equipment that you will need when the puppy first arrives (see Chapter Four: The New Arrival). Secondly, there will be routine veterinary fees, such as worming, parasite prevention, vaccinations, costs of neutering (if desired), identification, such as a microchip, and the costs of a pet passport if you are thinking of taking your Shepherd abroad on holiday. Unforeseen veterinary expenses caused by illness or accident can be taken care of by insuring your Shepherd. Obviously the insurance premium, along with any excess is an added expense. Puppy socialisation and training classes are important, so must also be considered.

Other expenses include making the garden secure. This means it will need to be fully fenced up to a level of around 5 ft (1.5 metres) with secure gates. If your puppy

The German Shepherd is a highly intelligent dog and he may become noisy or destructive if he is not given an outlet for his mental energies.

is likely to be unattended in a garden that is not completely safe, for even a few moments, you may need to consider fencing off a small portion or building a puppy run. If you are thinking of having an outside kennel and run, you will need to buy one that is of good quality and draught proof. However, it must be remembered that the German Shepherd likes to be with his family and will be very unhappy if left alone in a kennel for long periods.

The family car needs to be big enough to accommodate a large dog, so an estate car may be necessary if you have a family.

This all involves considerable financial outlay, so serious thought must be given to this aspect of owning a German Shepherd.

FAMILY SITUATION

Purchasing a German Shepherd must be a decision agreed by all of the family members. The new puppy will have some effect on the routines of everyone in the house. House rules and training commands for the new puppy must be agreed and all family members must adhere to them,

Do not under-estimate the amount of work you need to put into rearing a puppy.

otherwise the puppy will become confused.

Hours of work must be considered, as the new puppy will require almost constant care and attention. Popping home or arranging someone to visit at lunchtime is not satisfactory. Toilet training will be that much harder, or even impossible, if the puppy is left for long periods, and socialisation and training will be neglected. The puppy will become bored and possibly noisy, causing aggravation to the neighbours. A bored puppy is also likely to be destructive, resulting in some extensive damage to the home. A

German Shepherd thrives on companionship and is therefore not suitable in a home where all the family are working full-time.

Children must be taught to respect the new puppy; he is not a new toy and rough-and-tumble games must be firmly discouraged. A child who is frightened of dogs may find a puppy intimidating, as the puppy may chase and nip if the child squeals or runs away. Children should be taught to remain calm around the new puppy and avoid getting too excited. The German Shepherd is good with children, but they must be taught to have a mutual respect for each other.

CARE AND EXERCISE

When you take on a German Shepherd you are responsible for all his needs. These include:

FEEDING

You will need to feed a good-quality diet, regulating the amount you feed as your Shepherd grows.

• Do not allow your Shepherd to become overweight. A lean dog is likely to be much fitter and healthier than his obese counterpart. You should be able to feel all his ribs easily, but not see them.

- Do not allow your dog vigorous exercise for at least one hour before feeding and allow two hours after feeding, otherwise the risks of bloat and gastric torsion are increased (see Chapter Eight: Happy and Healthy).
- Do not allow your dog to be possessive of his food. Try adding a few more morsels of food to his bowl while he is feeding, so he welcomes your interference.

GROOMING

A German Shepherd needs regular grooming and this should start from the time a puppy arrives in his new home. Remember that long-coated Shepherds require grooming two or three times a week to prevent the coat from becoming matted.

EXERCISE

The new puppy will require very little exercise, apart from playing in the garden. It is important to take him out for socialisation purposes in the first few weeks, so you may have to carry him part of the way. Between 12 weeks and six months, he will still require little formal exercise; gradually increase the amount after six months until he is a year old; after which it may be unlimited.

HOLIDAYS

Consideration must be given to future holiday plans. Possibly a family friend may look after your Shepherd whilst you are away. Boarding kennels or the services of a house sitter are obvious solutions, but can be quite costly and usually have to be booked well in advance during 'peak' times.

Perhaps you are planning to take your Shepherd on holiday with you? There are plenty of places to go where dogs are welcome, although dogs are prohibited from many beaches in the UK during the summer months. The introduction of the Pet Passport has made it possible to take your pet abroad on holiday. The Pet Passport Scheme (PETS) means that pet dogs and cats that are resident in the UK can enter or re-enter the country without quarantine provided they meet the rules of PETS. Obtaining a pet passport is a fairly lengthy process, as it involves a rabies vaccination and subsequent blood tests.

It is a great bonus if you can take your German Shepherd on holiday with you.

GREAT EXPECTATIONS

Before you reserve a puppy from a breeder, you will need to decide what you want from your puppy. Do you just require a family pet, or are you hoping to show or work him?

All potential owners hope that their puppy matures to lead a long and healthy life, which unfortunately is impossible to guarantee. A puppy that is healthy at eight weeks of age may develop an unforeseen health condition later in life, which may be genetic or environmental. The risks are minimised by going to a reputable breeder, who will only breed from sound, healthy stock.

Most owners want a loyal, well-behaved companion with a good temperament. Of course, everyone wants a good-looking dog, but looks are generally of secondary importance, as long as the dog is typical of the breed in that he looks like a German Shepherd with erect ears. Faults that would make him totally unsuitable for showing, such as an undescended testicle or an overshot mouth, do not matter to the majority of pet owners, and minor faults, such as a steep croup or flat withers, would probably go unnoticed.

You may have ambitions to work your German Shepherd.

WORKING DOGS

Maybe you would also like to work your Shepherd? He is, of course, primarily a working dog with exceptional scenting ability, so excels at working trials. This includes searching and tracking, as well as basic obedience, climbing and jumping. It is a time-consuming sport, especially if it is done at competition level, requiring a lot of time and dedication to training.

Similar to working trials, the sport of Schutzhund (German for 'protection dog') was developed in Germany to test the working and protection ability of the German Shepherd. It is a demanding test and requires total control from an experienced and dedicated handler.

Obedience and agility are other options and, although the Shepherd may not be as quick as the Border Collie, he is a popular choice of breed in these competitions. Working a Shepherd is extremely rewarding and a very special bond forms between the dog and his handler.

SHOW DOGS

Perhaps you want to show your Shepherd? If this is the case, it is worth going to a few breed Championship shows, where you will see the better dogs exhibited. If you like the appearance of certain dogs, go and chat to their owners; they are usually more than happy to show you their 'pride and joy'. Showing a Shepherd is quite different to showing any other breed; they have to be extremely fit, very alert and willing to 'gait' for long periods.

There is also a variation in type in the German Shepherd in the UK, and attending various shows will give you an idea of the differences between individual dogs. The 'international' type of dog is the one described in the

Breed Standard. He is more athletic and is capable of winning worldwide, whereas the 'English' type (a term used by some breeders) is of longer body proportions, with a deeper chest and shorter legs. Joining a breed club in your area would be a good plan; this will give you some insight into the training and handling of the show dog as well as the opportunity of meeting breeders who may have promising puppies available.

MALE OR FEMALE?

The decision between a male or a female puppy needs to be made. This is largely a matter of personal preference, as, with the correct upbringing, both sexes make loyal companions and are good with children. The female is smaller and usually less dominant, so she may be slightly easier for the first-time Shepherd owner.

However, a female will come into season on average every six months, but it can vary from as often as every four to as infrequent as every nine months. At such times she may be a little 'hormonal' and will also need to be kept away from male dogs,

The male (right) is a bigger, stronger animal and needs more experienced handling than the female (left).

otherwise you may end up with an unwanted litter. Spaying (neutering) is an obvious option if you do not intend to breed from your Shepherd. I believe this is best performed approximately 12 weeks after her first or second season so she has had time to develop. Spaying before a first season may have the advantage of preventing mammary tumours and pyometra later in life, although it has the disadvantages of causing delayed fusion of the epiphyseal growth plates and a higher incidence of hip dysplasia, along with the

possibilities of urinary incontinence and an infantile vulva, which in turn leads to recurrent infections.

Careful thought must be given prior to the operation as, once performed, it is irreversible. Bitches which have been spayed often develop a rather 'woolly' coat texture and have a tendency to gain weight, so you may need to adhere to a strict diet.

The male is bigger, stronger and often more dominant, so can prove a handful for a weak or totally inexperienced owner. He will not come into season, so you will not have the inconvenience of having to cope with that, but he may cock his leg on inappropriate objects, such as garden chairs or tubs of flowers, as he marks his territory! It is possible to have him castrated (neutered) if he is becoming too dominant or showing signs of being oversexed, such as mounting people or marking inside the house. Castration is best performed around 12 months of age, after he has finished growing.

COAT AND COLOUR

Colour is varied in the German Shepherd and you may have a

The coat of a black and gold puppy will change as the gold spreads, leaving a black saddle.

A longcoated puppy has a softer, fluffier coat.

preference for a particular colour. The colours permitted by the Breed Standard are solid black; bi-colour; black with tan, gold, fawn or pale grey markings (the amount of black in relation to the gold can vary tremendously); and grey with darker, lighter or brown markings (known as sable).

A black and gold puppy may appear very dark when he is six weeks old, but he will get lighter when he grows his adult coat, as the gold spreads, leaving a black saddle. It is difficult to forecast how much black the puppy will retain as an adult, except in the case of an all-black or a bi-colour where the colour will not change.

Sable puppies are grey or sandy in colour at six weeks but they will get darker when they grow their adult coat. This starts with a black ring around the tail and a black stripe along the back, before spreading to cover the rest of the back and tail. Seeing the parents should give you some indication of the final colour.

White, blue or liver coat colours are not acceptable within the Breed Standard and any reputable breeder would exclude them from their breeding plans. Beware of any breeder selling so-called 'rare' puppies with incorrect colour at inflated prices.

Coat length should also be considered, as there may be normal (short) and long-coated puppies in a litter. Two normal-coated parents can produce a proportion of long-coated puppies, so you should inform the breeder of your preference. Long-coated puppies have noticeably fluffier and softer fur at six weeks. The long-coated Shepherd is attractive, but it is a fault within the Breed Standard and, as such, cannot be shown. A long-coated Shepherd is, however, perfectly suitable as a pet or a working dog, but remember that he requires more grooming and it takes longer to get him clean and dry after a wet, muddy walk!

The sable coat starts to darken with a black stripe along the back.

A sable pup will have a sandy or a grey coat.

FINDING A BREEDER

Assuming you have decided that that the German Shepherd is the right breed for your circumstances, the next step is to find a reputable breeder. Your local or the national breed club, or GSD breed council will be able to provide you with a list of breeders (see Appendices). The breed council in the UK has a 'breeders' charter,' which encourages good breeding and rearing practices, as well as strict guidelines for health checks, the number of puppies bred in a set period (no more than eight litters or 60 puppies in two years) and after-sales care.

The Kennel Club (KC) can also provide a list of breeders with puppies available. However,

puppies advertised as 'Kennel Club Registered' is not enough to guarantee that they have been bred by an ethical breeder. The UK Kennel Club will still register puppies, even if the parents do not have the recommended health checks. Introduction of the Kennel Club Accredited Breeders scheme is designed to encourage reputable breeders. Accredited breeders must adhere to the KC code of ethics, identify all breeding stock by means of DNA testing, microchip or tattoo and carry out compulsory health checks, which in this breed is hip scoring and haemophilia testing. Elbow scoring and eye checks are recommended but, as yet, are not mandatory. The scheme is not foolproof and you would be

advised to examine the results of any health checks, as accredited breeders can still register a litter even if the results are well outside the recommended guidelines stipulated by the breed council, and regardless of how many litters are bred by a particular kennel.

Beware of answering an advert in the local paper, unless you can be sure the advertiser is genuine. Buying from a pet shop or an establishment that has many breeds for sale is not recommended, as they often buy puppies or whole litters to sell on, purely for financial gain without any regard for temperament, health or bloodlines. These puppies are usually taken away from their

CHECKLIST

Once you have a list of breeders, you will need to make contact to ensure the following criteria:

- You should be able to meet all of the dogs, especially the mother of the puppies and any other relatives. This will give you an idea of how the puppy will turn out. It is not always possible to meet the father, as the breeder may have travelled some distance to find a suitable mate for the bitch.

- Both parents should have had the required health checks with satisfactory results. Both parents should be hip scored with the certificates available for you to see if so requested. The sire of the litter should be tested for haemophilia A, with a negative result. Many breeders also have the elbows X-rayed and scored and although not compulsory in the UK, it is recommended.

- The puppies should be registered with the national kennel club. Some breeders choose to have the KC registration endorsed, to protect the puppy and the breed. The endorsements available are: a) 'progeny not eligible for registration' and b) 'not eligible for the issue of an export pedigree.' If you plan to breed from your puppy in the future, you will need to find out what criteria are required before the breeder will lift the endorsement.

- The puppies should be sold with a sales agreement, which gives you the opportunity to have the puppy checked by a veterinary surgeon within a specified number of days after purchase. If any defects are found, you should have the option of returning the puppy to the breeder. Any restrictions on breeding or export should be covered along with any plans for reimbursement should the puppy die from an inherited condition in the first year. The agreement should also stipulate what should happen to the dog, should he need to be re-homed at any stage during his lifetime. All ethical breeders will assist with re-homing or even take the dog back.

- The puppies should be tattooed in the ear or microchipped for identification purposes. Many breeders also have the litter checked by a vet prior to placing them in their new homes.

Take time to find a suitable breeder who produces sound, healthy, typical German Shepherds.

mother too early, inadequately socialised and often sickly.

You are about to make an addition to your family, who will be a companion for the next 10 or 12 years. Therefore you would be well advised to go to an experienced and genuine breeder; one who has a good knowledge of the breed and who will be happy to help and advise you throughout the dog's life. You should feel able to call on them for advice several years down the line if necessary, so a good relationship with the breeder is essential.

VISITING A BREEDER

A genuine breeder needs to be sure that you will be a suitable owner for one of their puppies, so you should be asked some searching questions before your name is added to any waiting list. If you are not asked any questions, it may be that the breeder does not actually care where the puppy is going. Once you have found a breeder, you will need to find out when their next litter is due. You may have to reserve a puppy in advance, as many reputable breeders will have most of the

litter booked before they are born, so arrange to visit the kennel before the litter is due. Do not visit more than one breeder on the same day, as infection can be transferred on shoes and clothing from kennel to kennel.

Most breeders are proud of their dogs and will be happy for you to meet the whole 'family'. Being a fairly vocal breed, the dogs will probably bark when you arrive and then greet you with wagging tails. They should not be on a lead or the other side of a fence, nor should they growl or shy away from you. The dogs should be happy and outgoing and appear clean and healthy, without any unpleasant odour.

The breeder should be happy to give you a tour of the kennels and show you where the puppies will be born and raised, all of which should be scrupulously clean. Ideally the puppies will be born and reared in a home environment, where they will be accustomed to the noises and 'hustle and bustle' of people, children and other dogs, as well as household appliances such as the vacuum cleaner, washing machine and television. If the weather permits, an outside playpen for use in the daytime is ideal where the puppies can safely romp and play. Puppies which are reared solely in outside kennels and not exposed to everyday experiences will lack the initial socialisation that is very important in this breed.

Do not be afraid to ask questions, the breeder should be more than happy to assist you in

You will want to see the mother with her puppies, as this will give you some idea of the temperament they are likely to inherit.

your search for the right puppy. It is imperative that you choose a breeder that you trust and with whom you feel comfortable, so do not commit yourself to buying a puppy until you feel that this is the case. You should not feel as though you are being rushed into making a decision to buy a puppy, nor should you be asked for any deposit until after the litter is born.

VIEWING THE LITTER
The breeder will inform you if there is a puppy available for you once the litter has been born. You will no doubt be anxious to see the puppies as soon as possible, but don't be surprised if you are not allowed to visit before the puppies are three or four weeks old. There is very little to see before this; the puppies will spend all of their time suckling from their mother or sleeping, and the dam will only have eyes for her babies. I usually take photographs each week so that prospective owners can see the litter as they grow.

When you do visit, make sure you are wearing clean clothes and shoes and have not been in contact with any other dogs. You may be asked to remove your shoes and wash your hands to minimise the risk of any infection being passed to the puppies. It is important to see the mother with her puppies; she may keep a watchful eye over her babies but she should not be aggressive towards you.

Children must be supervised with the puppies at all times.

They should sit on the floor to play with them and not be allowed to pick them up. Puppies can be very 'wriggly' and would easily be dropped by a child, resulting in possible injury. The litter should be clean and bright-eyed with clean ears, and the area in which they are reared should be fresh and hygienic. Steer clear of pot-bellied puppies on fine spindly legs, as this indicates a poorly reared litter or the presence of worms.

The puppies should be lively, playful and inquisitive and bound up to you without any signs of nervousness. Their bodies should be firm, well covered and feel heavier than they look, but not fat and 'roly-poly'. A healthy litter may get a brief tummy upset during weaning, but otherwise their motions should be firm and well formed.

ASSESSING THE PUPPIES
Whether you are looking for a puppy for showing, working or as a family pet, the ideal time at which to choose your puppy is around the age of six weeks, when character and conformation is becoming more evident

THE IDEAL PET PUPPY
Unless you have any particular preference for colour or coat, which will obviously limit your choice, you would be wise to choose the puppy with the most suitable temperament. Most breeders will spend many hours observing and playing with the

A puppy with working potential should be responsive and eager to play.

The breeder will help 'stand up' a puppy to help you assess show potential.

litter, so do be guided as to which puppy is best for your requirements. For instance, the quiet, sensitive puppy may be overwhelmed if placed in a lively household with lots of children. Choose a puppy that is friendly, fearless and comes to you when you make an encouraging sound. An ideal pet puppy is one that is happy for you to pick him up or handle him.

- Be careful not to choose an overly bold puppy (known as the alpha). He will be the one who rushes up to you first and maybe tugs on your sleeve. You may think that he has chosen you, but in fact he will do this to everyone. He may object to being restrained or beat up his littermates. This puppy may be a constant challenge in the average pet home, so is best left to an experienced handler.

- Avoid any puppy that cowers in the corner or one that jumps at the slightest sound. A shy puppy needs a very experienced owner, who will help him overcome his fears.

Any obvious faults, such as an undescended testicle, umbilical hernia or an overshot mouth, should be pointed out by a conscientious breeder, although these faults will not make the dog an unsuitable companion. Some puppies are born with dew claws on the hind legs, so do check they have been removed, although they are left intact on the front legs in this breed.

POTENTIAL WORKING ABILITY
Should you wish to work your Shepherd, whether in obedience, working trials, schutzhund or agility, you will need to choose a puppy with certain criteria. Ask to see the puppy away from his littermates and ideally in an area unfamiliar to him.

He will need to be alert, lively, outgoing and inquisitive. A puppy that sits quietly, uninterested in what is going on, may make a calm, laidback pet, but he will not be a keen working dog.

- He should be responsive, so call him to you by making an encouraging sound.

- See if he will pick up and carry different articles. Try throwing a piece of scrunched-up paper; if he picks it up, encourage him back to you. You could also try a bunch of keys, as they are noisy and some dogs have an aversion to picking up metal.

- If you have a large piece of rag or similar, pull it along the floor. If he pounces on it and then tugs at it, then he has the ability to develop pronounced 'prey drive'.

- Do not choose any puppy that is unresponsive or oblivious to your efforts to interact with him. Avoid the puppy that jumps when a sudden noise is made, such as a loud bang or clapping your hands, as this puppy may be oversensitive to sound.

THE POTENTIAL SHOW DOG
It is impossible to guarantee that an eight-week-old puppy with show potential will make a successful show dog. Some do go on to fulfil that early promise, but many more don't make the grade.

If you are inexperienced, you would be well advised to take a knowledgeable breeder with you, or go to an established and successful breeder and outline your intentions.

Watch the puppies trotting around and choose one that is alert and confident – one that holds his shape whilst moving, keeping a firm backline that slopes gently from front to back. The puppy will need to be stood on a non-slip surface for you to assess his shape in more detail and, at six to eight weeks, he should resemble a miniature version of the adult he will become. Therefore, proportions of height to length and angulations fore and aft should be correct. Ideally, the ears will have started to lift at the base and the bite should be correct. However, teeth are notoriously difficult to forecast and occasionally a promising puppy will develop a tooth fault, which, in this breed, will put an end to a show career. A male puppy should have a masculine head and stronger bone than a bitch puppy and also two testicles descended into the scrotum.

The alternative is to buy an older puppy in excess of six months of age, which has perhaps been 'run on' with a couple of other littermates. This option is not so much of a gamble, as the teeth and ears will be correct by this time, and the hips may have already been screened. Of course, you will have to pay more money or, if the puppy is female, some breeders

It is vitally important that breeding stock is screened for inherited diseases.

will sell her on 'breeding terms'. This will keep the initial outlay lower, but if you do agree to these terms, make sure there is a written contract to avoid any misunderstandings in the future.

HEALTH CHECKS
There are a number of health checks the breeder should have carried out on breeding stock.

HIPS
Hip scoring schemes are available in many countries where the hip joints and pelvis are X-rayed and evaluated for any evidence of hip dysplasia. The minimum age for having the hips X-rayed and assessed is 12 months, except in the United States where the minimum age is 24 months.

In the UK the hips are X-rayed by a veterinary surgeon and the plates are submitted to the British Veterinary Association (BVA) for 'hip-scoring'. The lower the total score indicates, the better hip conformation. Each hip can score from 0 (best) to a maximum of 53 (worst), and the 'hip score' is the total of each hip added together. Therefore the best possible score is 0:0 and the worst 53:53. The average hip score for the German Shepherd is at present a total of 19. Ideally, the sire and dam of the litter should have hip scores of less than the breed average.

In the United States the hip-scoring scheme is supported by the Orthopaedic Foundation for Animals (OFA). A grade of excellent, good or fair is required for the hips to be considered within normal limits and given an OFA certificate and identification number. Radiographs considered to be borderline, mild, moderate and severely dysplastic are reviewed by the OFA radiologist and the abnormal radiographic findings are documented.

In Germany and Europe hip scoring is recognised by Verein für Deutsche Schäferhunde (SV) and Fédération Cynologique Internationale (FCI), respectively. The SV award an 'a' stamp when the hips are classed as normal, 'fast normal' (nearly normal) and 'noch zugelassen' (acceptable). A dog with an 'a' stamp is deemed suitable for breeding. In Europe A1 and A2 are considered normal and B1 and B2 are considered fair or near normal with transitional changes.

Although hip dysplasia is considered a hereditary condition, it must be remembered that environmental factors, such as excess weight or over-exercise, can greatly influence the problem.

HAEMOPHILIA A
This is a sex-linked inherited condition affecting German Shepherd males, where the blood is unable to clot, causing uncontrollable bleeding. All male Shepherds should therefore be tested and certified clear of the condition prior to being used at stud.

It may suit your lifestyle to take on an older dog.

ELBOWS
Elbow dysplasia is a common condition affecting many large breeds, including the German Shepherd. Elbow-scoring schemes exist to assess the degree of abnormality present, which enables breeders to ensure their breeding stock is free from the condition. It is similar to the hip-scoring scheme, although the range of scores in the UK is 0-3, with 0 being the best (free from any dysplasia), and 3 being the most severe. It is not mandatory to have the elbows scored in the

UK, but it is recommended. As with hip dysplasia it is not a simple inherited condition, but is influenced by several genetic factors, known as a polygenic trait.

EYE TESTING
An eye testing scheme exists in the UK, supported by the BVA and KC where the eyes may be tested for the presence of hereditary cataracts. It is an uncommon condition in this breed, and although eye tests are promoted by the Kennel Club, it is not yet mandatory.

TAKING ON AN OLDER OR RESCUED DOG
There are always German Shepherds of all ages in need of a new home. Some are puppies of only a few months old, which usually find new homes quickly; whilst others are elderly Shepherds needing a comfortable and loving home where they can spend their last days – and sadly, these are the ones that are often overlooked.

An older Shepherd will obviously take longer to settle into a new home than an eight-week-old puppy, so you will need patience and understanding. It is imperative that you know what you will be taking on, as some of these dogs may have had a traumatic time and are in need of a permanent and stable home.

If you think you would like to take on a rescued dog, you would be well advised to go to a rescue centre that specialises in German Shepherds, or a reputable all-breed rescue centre. Here you will be 'vetted' to ensure that your home, and your family situation, are suitable for an older dog. This is important, as some dogs may not be reliable with children, with other dogs, or with cats. The staff will be experienced in this breed and will be able to assess a Shepherd's character and temperament and work out how he reacts with adults, children and other animals. It is important to know the history of the dog: for instance whether he has any ongoing health or temperament problems and the reasons for him being re-homed. There are legitimate reasons for rehoming, such as family break-ups, owners moving abroad, illness or bereavement. However, many Shepherds are put into rescue due to a behavioural

If you work at training and socialising your German Shepherd, you will have a companion that is second to none.

problem, such as destructiveness, nervousness or aggression. If this type of dog is to be re-homed, he needs an owner with much experience of the breed. As discussed earlier in the chapter, the German Shepherd is a 'high maintenance' breed and needs plenty of training and socialising during his formative months, and, sadly, there are plenty of irresponsible breeders who will sell puppies to unsuitable homes.

Once you have found a dog

suitable for you, you will be asked to make a donation. A higher donation will normally be required for a younger dog. Most rescue centres rely heavily on donations to fund the daily running costs and veterinary care.

Sometimes a breeder may have an older dog available, perhaps one that has been 'run on' for the show ring, but hasn't quite made the grade, or one that has been used for breeding and is now retired. In these cases you will need to find out whether the dog has been socialised adequately with children and other animals, and whether the dog is used to living in the house. Occasionally, an older dog will become available, which was sold as a puppy and is returned because of a legitimate reason, as most reputable breeders will take back dogs of their own breeding.

SUMMING UP

Whether you decide on a puppy or an older dog, be sure that you have the time and commitment to give to this wonderful breed. You are about to acquire a very dear friend, who will give you loyalty and devotion second to none.

THE NEW ARRIVAL

Before you collect your puppy or rescued dog, there are a number of preparations to make. If you plan ahead, you will give your German Shepherd the best possible chance of settling in his new home.

IN THE HOME

The first decision to make is where to locate your German Shepherd's bed. The majority of owners opt for the kitchen or utility room, but make sure that the location allows your German Shepherd to escape from the bustle of family life when he wants.

If you do not wish to allow him access to the entire house, a child gate is very useful to keep him in certain rooms or from going upstairs. A puppy's bones take a long time to fully form, so it is best not to allow him to put any strain on them by going up and down stairs. The same applies to allowing him to jump on and off furniture – which may not be desirable in any case. You need to set the house rules from day one; it is no use saying: "He can do it now, but later on when he is bigger I don't want him to." A dog will have no idea why the rules have changed and will begin to doubt your authority.

Try to see your home from a puppy's perspective and think about what may attract his attention: shoes, children's toys, books, wires – the possibilities are endless. The golden rule is to keep anything that is potentially hazardous – or valuable – out of his reach. As your German Shepherd grows taller, you will have to check the house again. He will be at just the right height for jumping up at food counters, so make sure this is discouraged from an early stage.

IN THE GARDEN

Once you are confident that your house is safe, turn your attention to the garden. Is it well fenced? Are your fences high enough to confine a fully-grown German Shepherd? Make sure that you have a lock on the gate so that it cannot be opened accidentally. Check that you do not have any plants that may be poisonous to a dog (there are good lists available on the internet), and ensure there are no dangerous areas with glass, wire, or any other sort of rubbish. Garden products such as pesticides should be safely locked away; this also applies to car products, such as oil, fuel or anti-freeze. A puppy tests everything with his mouth and can all too easily ingest a substance that could make him very ill, or even kill him.

If you have a good-sized garden, you may want to consider a kennel with a run

German Shepherd puppies are great explorers, so check out your garden for potential hazards.

where he can enjoy the fresh air but be sheltered from sun or rain. Again, consider his adult size and give him sufficient room. If your Shepherd learns to stay in his kennel quietly, perhaps with another dog if you have one, then he can be safely left if you have to go out or if you have visitors who are not keen on dogs.

Always remember to leave fresh water in the run. A German Shepherd who is used to a kennel and run will be quite happy to stay there for short periods and watch you while you mow the grass or have a barbecue.

BUYING EQUIPMENT
There are a few essential items on the shopping list, and it is useful

to get these before your German Shepherd arrives home.

CRATE
This is an invaluable piece of equipment, and your Shepherd will love it too, looking upon it as a safe den where he can go with his chews, toys, or just have a quiet nap away from the rest of the household.

You will need to ensure that the crate you buy will be big enough for an adult German Shepherd to stand, stretch and turn around in comfortably. The average adult will require a crate 49 x 30.5 x 33.5 inches (1.25 x 0.75 x 0.85 metres).

DOG BED
In addition to a crate, you may

want to buy a dog bed so that your German Shepherd has another base he can use when you are in the sitting room or elsewhere. There are lots of different beds to choose from, ranging from bean bags and duvets to wicker baskets. The most practical choice is a plastic bed, which can be lined with cosy bedding. Again, make sure the bed you buy is big enough for a fully-grown Shepherd to stretch out in comfort.

FOOD AND WATER BOWLS
There are many different bowls to choose from, but the most durable are those made of stainless steel. These are virtually indestructible and they are also easy to keep clean.

GROOMING GEAR
You will need brushes and combs to keep your German Shepherd's coat in good order. I would advise a stiff bristle brush, a slicker brush and a roller comb (which has revolving metal teeth that tease out any knots or matts). Grooming should be a pleasant experience that furthers the bond between dog and owner, so make sure you spend time getting your dog accustomed to the brushes, and use food rewards when your Shepherd behaves well. If your dog's coat is in a particularly bad condition, you would be better advised to seek the help of a professional groomer.

COLLARS AND LEADS
Remember that your puppy will

CRATE TRAINING

Crate training should begin from an early age so that your puppy learns to stay quietly in there when you have to nip out to the shops, or if you are going to be busy for a short time and cannot keep an eye on him. The big advantage of a crate is that a puppy is safely confined and cannot get up to mischief or harm while you are away. If you have visitors who do not appreciate a dog's attentions, the pup can go in his crate with a nice treat until they leave.

Initially, line the crate with some bedding (e.g. bankets, fleece bedding or vetbed, etc.). You are likely to get through quite a lot of beedding with a young puppy, so don't choose anything too expensive and make sure your puppy cannot chew it up, swallow itt and make himself ill. Put some toys in the crate so the puppy gets used to going in and out of it, with the door open. Feeding your puppy in the crate will help to reinforce the feel-good factor. When he has had a really good play, emptied himself, and is feeling tired, put him in the crate with a chew or a biscuit, and then shut the door. The puppy will probably protest a little but, being tired, he will soon fall asleep. When he wakes up, take him straight outside to do his business.

A crate is a very useful training aid, but a puppy should never be left in it for more than a couple of hours at a time during the course of the day. Make sure you wait until the puppy is quiet before letting him out of the crate, or he will associate barking with getting your attention. Most crates are collapsible and can be folded away when not in use.

After a while you can dispense with the crate once your puppy has stopped chewing and can be trusted when he is unsupervised. However, most adult Shepherds are more than happy to have a crate at their disposal.

It does not take long before a puppy looks on a crate as his own special den.

grow very quickly, so, initially, an adjustable collar is the best choice. However, you may find that a half-check collar, which has a chain insert, will give you more control when you are training. Choose a lead that is strong but is also comfortable for you. Nylon leads can cut your hands if your Shepherd pulls suddenly; chain leads are terrible on your hands, and can hurt your dog. The best-quality leather leads and collars will last you years if they are oiled regularly, but it is best not to invest in these while your puppy is still at the chewing stage.

Show leads and collars are of a different type, so seek specialist advice if you plan to show your German Shepherd.

ID

Your German Shepherd must have some form of identification.

You can get a disc, engraved with your address and telephone number, which is attached to your dog's collar. You may also want to consider a form of permanent ID. Some breeders have their puppies tattooed in the ear, but this cannot always be read easily once the dog becomes an adult. The other option is to have your puppy microchipped, which provides a safe and permanent form of ID.

TOYS

There is a huge variety of toys available for your dog, but you must give consideration to your German Shepherd's size and strength. Some toys are easily destroyed, and most will carry a warning that a dog should not be left unattended while playing with the toy.

Safe toys are large tuggers,

made from knotted rope, which Shepherds find good to chew, especially when teething. Large hard, rubber balls or a strong football are also popular toys. Invariably your Shepherd will burst the football, but he will still have hours of fun carrying it around. Beware of soft toys with glass eyes, and watch out for squeaky toys – puppies are adept at removing the 'squeak', sometimes with disastrous consequences. You will also need to watch out for those pups with a fetish for stealing your washing, as a sock can cause a nasty blockage; the same applies to plastic bags.

Check your German Shepherd's toys regularly to make sure that he isn't biting pieces off and swallowing them. If you are vigilant, you can make use of a plastic bottle, with the top and ring removed. This can provide your Shepherd with hours of cheap fun and is easily replaced. Sticks can be very dangerous, especially if thrown and he catches it long-ways.

FOOD

Check with your breeder what food he has been reared on and make sure that you can get it easily, or arrange for it to be delivered. If you wish to change to another puppy food, make sure that this is done gradually to accustom him to it. Mix it with the food that he was reared on and slowly increase the new food, while decreasing the 'old' food, until a complete changeover is complete.

Check toys on a regular basis to make sure they are still safe to play with.

TREATS

Treats come in all sorts of flavours, shapes and sizes, but do remember that these have nutritional value. They should not be fed *ad lib*, but accounted for in your dog's daily rations.

Beef bones can be given; a marrow bone is best, but always make sure they cannot be easily splintered, and remove any small pieces that could be dangerous if swallowed. These can be fed raw.

You can also buy roasted or smoked bones from your pet shop. Remove them once they get too small. Never feed chicken, turkey, lamb or pork bones, which splinter easily and can pierce a dog's intestines if swallowed. Similarly, hide chews are sometimes dangerous if large pieces are swallowed, which can happen where there is competition between dogs. I give my puppies large carrots to play with; if they chew them and eat them, they will be digested and not cause any problems.

FINDING A VET

Before you collect your puppy, find a reputable vet in your area and arrange for an appointment so your pup can be checked over. The pup may need his vaccination, and you can also discuss worming procedures. You can also have a microchip inserted in his neck for ID purposes if this has not already been done.

Ask at your local vet or pet shops where there are training classes for socialisation, ringcraft or obedience. Even if you never

Generally, a breeder will allow puppies to go to their new homes when they are around eight weeks old.

intend to compete or show your German Shepherd, it is essential that he learns to mix with other dogs and has a solid grounding in manners. He will grow into a large dog who must be under control at all times if he is not to be a nuisance to your neighbours and general public. A well-trained dog is a pleasure to own and is happy into the bargain. Enrolling into a basic puppy class will ensure that he learns to behave before he gets too big for you to control. See Chapter Six: Training and Socialisation.

COLLECTING YOUR PUPPY

So now you have everything ready and the day has come to collect your new puppy. I ask new owners to come early in the morning, so that the puppy has plenty of time to get used to his new home before it is time for him to spend his first night away from his littermates. It is also a good idea if the pup is collected at a weekend, or when you have booked some time off work, so that you have time to help your puppy settle in.

Before you take your puppy

away, make sure that you have been given all the relevant paperwork:

- Kennel Club registration documents: These should be signed by the breeder, and you then send them to the Kennel Club to transfer ownership.
- Contract: The breeder will draw up a contract, stating the terms or conditions of the sale.
- A record of worming treatments: I supply the next two worming doses and also state which wormer I have used and the dates they were administered.
- Diet sheet: This gives information about the type of food and quantities required as the puppy grows.
- Food: Most breeders supply a small amount of the food the puppy has been reared on, in order to avoid digestive upset in the first few days.

Make sure that the puppy you have chosen looks healthy and is lively and outgoing. Most breeders have their puppies checked by a vet prior to being sold. Take the opportunity to ask relevant questions about grooming, feeding, and training. A responsible breeder will be only too happy to give you advice, both at the time of sale and in the weeks and months ahead, should problems arise.

CLEAN UP!

You need to buy the means to clean up after your dog. This can take the form of a pooper scooper and poo bags, or you may find you can manage with poo bags alone.

When you travel home, make sure you have someone to supervise the puppy when you are driving. Place the puppy in the footwell of the vehicle or in a crate with plenty of newspapers. Come equipped with towels, and be prepared to make a stop if the puppy is sick and you need to clean him up.

ARRIVING HOME

It is natural for everyone to be excited by the arrival of a new puppy, but try not to let him get overawed with crowds of people who want to hug him. Children must learn that he is not a toy, and they must allow him to explore his new surroundings quietly. See Playing with Children, page 62.

Remember that this will be the most traumatic day in your German Shepherd's life so far, and you must try to make it as stress-free as possible. He will be very busy exploring his new home and, hopefully, by the end of the day he will be tired and ready for a good night's sleep.

MEETING THE FAMILY PETS

If you have a resident dog, make sure that the new puppy does not get all the attention; he must learn his place in the hierarchy. An older dog must be reassured that he is still the most important, otherwise he may be jealous and attack the puppy at every opportunity. However, you should reprimand the older dog if he is too harsh in telling the puppy off; likewise, the puppy must be told off if he dares to challenge the older dog. It is important that your puppy recognises you as his pack leader and accepts your authority from day one.

At mealtimes, make sure the puppy is supervised so he does not attempt to steal the resident dog's food – or have his own food stolen. Your puppy is used to eating with his littermates, probably out of a communal bowl, so he must learn that he now has his own bowl and must respect older dogs. The same applies to favourite toys.

It is always best not to leave a puppy unsupervised with an older dog, especially where squabbles can arise over food or treats. Teach your puppy to give up his toys or bones to you. Initially he may growl or snap, so make sure he knows that he must not do this. One day, he may chew something harmful that you need to remove quickly.

HOUSE TRAINING

Remember that the puppy is only a few weeks old and he will not understand that he must go outside to do his toilet; this is something that you must teach him. The times he needs to be taken out are:

- On waking
- After eating
- After playing
- At hourly intervals if he has not been taken out at the times stated above.

You will soon learn to recognise the telltale signs when a puppy needs to 'go' and should be taken outside. Generally, a pup will become restless and start to circle. Under no circumstance should a puppy be scolded, or, worse still, have his nose rubbed in his urine or excreta if he makes a mistake. This is a disgusting practice and serves no useful purpose.

If you can catch your puppy at the point when he is about to relieve himself, say "No" firmly, pick him up and put him outside. He may be confused at first, but after watching him and praising him when he empties, using a phrase such as "Clean – good boy", he will soon associate the command with his actions.

If you are vigilant, your puppy will quickly get the idea of house training.

MEETING THE ANIMAL FAMILY

Make sure you give your resident dog plenty of attention while he is getting used to the newcomer.

In time, a German Shepherd and a cat will live in harmony with each other.

Initially your puppy will be curious about smaller animals, such as hamsters, and it is best to make sure that he does not have access to them. A firm "No!", with a hand in the dog's collar initially, will have to be repeated to make sure that your German Shepherd understands he must not touch them. Keeping small animals in a separate room and secure cages is the best approach.

The family cat may well avoid the new puppy or take a swipe with its claws. A firm "No" repeated regularly will normally suffice for the puppy to understand that he must not retaliate or give chase. It may be harder to enforce with an older dog who understands how fun chasing can be. If you are taking on an older dog, make sure you know if he is used to other animals and children.

MEALTIMES

Take your breeder's advice and feed your puppy little and often; at eight weeks of age he will usually need four, but possibly five, meals a day. You will find that as he grows he will regulate his appetite and you can reduce the number of feeds, but obviously the amounts will increase per meal. Feeding guides are on the packet of most dog foods but these may vary due to the amount of exercise given and an individual dog's metabolism; they are intended as guides only.

Make sure that fresh water is always available. Puppies do not need milk once they have been weaned from their mother; they cannot digest it properly and it causes tummy upsets.

THE FIRST NIGHT

If you want your puppy to sleep downstairs at night, make sure he does this from the very first night. Heartbreaking wails should be ignored; the puppy should soon grow tired and go to sleep. It is advisable to pre-warn your neighbours that you have a new addition and that he may be a little noisy until he settles in. Make sure that he has been fed and has been outside and done his business and had a little play. Then put him to bed with a cosy blanket and a chew – something safe that he can chomp on should he wake early.

Your puppy will let you know when he wants to get up in the morning, but be prepared to have a few accidents to clean up if you do not respond in time. I use a large crate with newspaper at the front and a bed at the back so that the puppy does not have to foul his sleeping quarters. Most dogs do not like to mess in their beds and will try very hard to wait until let out. He should be put straight outside, given his command to empty, be praised and then he can come in for his first meal.

REST AND PLAY

Puppies sleep a lot of the time at first, but they need less sleep as they get older. A young puppy needs to sleep in order to grow, and you must ensure that he has the opportunity to rest.

At eight weeks, a German Shepherd puppy will get sufficient exercise playing in the house and garden. He does not need to be taken out for long walks; his bones have a lot of growing and strengthening to do. This process takes many months, and it is important that a puppy does not put too much strain on his young joints. If he gets too much exercise, he will damage his bones forever – all too often, I see weedy dogs who have been over-exercised at a young age. I like to see puppies with a covering on their ribs – not overweight but not thin. Too much weight is as harmful as too much exercise.

HEALTH CHECK

Take your puppy to the vet within the first couple of days, making sure it is a nice experience for him. There will be strange sights and smells for him to encounter, so take some treats so that he associates this experience with food. Your vet will give the

A puppy is likely to feel bewildered when he first arrives in his new home.

FINDING TIME FOR YOUR PUPPY

A puppy should never have to be alone for more than a few hours at a time, which is, obviously, a major consideration before you even consider bringing a puppy into your life. Some people who go out to work all day arrange for a dog-sitter or neighbour to come in regularly and take the puppy out for walks and feed him, but this is not ideal. This is a very formative time of a puppy's life when you should be building a bond with him.

Nowadays a lot of people work from home, which is fine as long as you realise that you may not get quite so much work done when your puppy first arrives. However, do not fall into the trap of giving him attention all the time or he will come to expect it, and he may become stressed if he is left on his own. Organise a routine of times you will take him out, feed him, and times when he must rest – and this will help with the settling-in process.

puppy a thorough examination and may administer the first of two inoculations, depending on his age. Practices vary depending on the vet's policy and disease incidence in the area, but your puppy must not go out where other dogs have fouled until he

A puppy's mouth may be sore when he is teething, and, in the case of a German Shepherd puppy, ear carriage may be erratic.

has had both inoculations. However, this does not stop you from carrying your puppy so that he sees strange sights and sounds from the safety of your arms. Go to car boot sales and markets, or just sit in a park or shopping precinct so that he can look around and not be frightened. People will often stop to pet a small puppy, which is good for him, and you can reassure him should he be at all worried; a handful of treats always helps.

FIRST LESSONS

A young puppy has so much to learn, so start as you mean to go on and get to work teaching some important first lessons.

MOUTHING

Puppies use their teeth a lot in play, which often hurts, as they are very sharp. Your puppy must not be allowed to bite, as this can become a bigger problem as he grows up. A firm "No" should slow him down, but you will have to repeat this often. Do not tease him or encourage him to grab your clothes. Playing should always be under control and, if it gets out of hand, distract him with a treat or toy and end the game.

A puppy will shed his milk teeth at about four months old, so make sure he has plenty of toys to mouth on rather than your best furniture. His mouth will be very sore at this time and he may go off his food as he finds it painful to chew. I use a little Bonjela or Dentinox and rub it

into the gums to relieve the soreness.

Too much playing and tugging on toys may damage his adult teeth, which are still not firm in the jaw, so make sure that play time does not become too rough.

PLAYING WITH CHILDREN

If you have children, play can get a little out of hand as both puppy and children get excited. A little puppy sees his new friends as littermates, and he will jump up and grab their hands, clothes and toys. He is growing fast and will soon be big enough to knock over a child and leap on them. If the child cries or screams, pup will think it a fine game.

You need to teach the child to play, keeping the puppy on the floor. The puppy must not be allowed to jump on top of the child; this is a sign of dominance, which would be quite natural with his littermates to sort out a natural pecking order, but is not acceptable with humans. It is important to establish that children are above your puppy in the hierarchy of the family.

Children and dogs should always be supervised. Never let a child take the puppy out into the street on a lead on their own, as this may result in serious accidents. Your children's friends must also be educated around the puppy; remember that he is going to be a big dog and nowadays we live in an anti-dog society. If he jumps up and scratches another child's face or nips them, you may end up with an irate parent accusing you of owning a

Play sessions should always be supervised, but, with care and training, a German Shepherd will learn to behave calmly around children.

dangerous dog. At worst, this could result in court action, and you may be compelled to get rid of your dog or even have him put to sleep.

GREETING VISITORS

You must also teach your German Shepherd how to behave when people are invited into your home. He must accept when you tell him that they are allowed in. Some people do not like dogs, especially if the dog jumps up to greet them or jumps all over them when they sit down. You are aiming for a friendly dog who poses no danger to anyone.

GETTING USED TO A COLLAR AND LEAD

Put a light collar on your puppy for short periods of time so he becomes accustomed to having something round his neck. Do not grab his collar to chastise or catch him, as he will soon learn to evade you. Never leave a collar on when your puppy is playing at home, as it can easily get caught up on a bush or fence or act as a 'choker' if he is playing with another dog.

A German Shepherd's first experience of a lead being attached can be somewhat akin to a fish on a line: he may pull

backwards, panic and scream. Get down to his level and call him to you to reassure him. It is far better to attach the lead and let him drag it round after him at first, progressing to playing with a toy or letting him lead you as he goes to look at something new. Progress in easy stages, and always reward your puppy when he does as you ask.

You must have a lot of patience with your puppy, as he has had no constraints for the first eight weeks of his life, and you do not want him to become stressed or fearful. Once he has had his vaccinations, you can start with basic puppy classes. A well-trained dog is a happy dog with a proud owner. See Chapter Six: Training and Socialisation.

CAR TRAVEL

It is important to get your puppy used to travelling calmly in the car. It is best to have a crate in the back of the vehicle so that he feels secure and is not loose, jumping around and barking and perhaps causing you to have an accident. Some puppies are travel sick at first, but will generally grow out of it the more often they are taken out. Make sure you have plenty of newspaper to clean up should your puppy be sick, and provide bedding that prevents him from slipping about.

Your puppy must be discouraged from barking at passers-by, dogs and vehicles. Start by telling him "No" firmly and praising him when he is quiet. Sometimes it is necessary to resort to other means. Recruit a helper who can spray the dog with water from a spray bottle if he continues to bark after you have asked him to be "Quiet". As soon as the dog is quiet, give him lots of praise and the helper can give him a treat. In this way, he will learn that it is more rewarding for him to be quiet than to bark.

You can also teach your puppy to "Wait" while you open the door to let him out of the car. He must stay in position until you have clipped on his lead, and then you can give a command to jump out. This is a lesson in good manners, but it could also save his life if there are passing vehicles.

TAKING ON A RESCUED DOG

There are a lot of German Shepherds coming into rescue all the time, and taking on an older dog may be a suitable option if you do not have the time to raise a small puppy. However, a rescued dog can be as demanding – if not more so – than a puppy. You can find German Shepherd co-ordinators by contacting a breed club, or the Kennel Club has a list it can send you.

Taking on a rescued dog may be a totally different experience to starting off with a puppy, depending on the dog's past history. Some dogs have been abused, others neglected; there are those that have grown out of the appealing puppy stage and are no longer wanted now they need training. Some Shepherds may have been destructive or noisy due to boredom from being left all day without any company. There are other reasons for rehoming a dog, such as a marriage break-up, bereavement,

You need to teach your German Shepherd to settle quietly in the car.

Time and patience are required to help a rescued dog settle into a new home.

or a house move.

When a dog comes in for rehoming, rescue workers try to find out as much background as possible, to assess the dog and to find a suitable home. However, there are some cases when a dog is found and nothing is known about his past.

SETTLING IN
A lot of the advice given about taking on a new puppy applies equally to rehoming an older dog.

But you may need to tackle additional problems, such as separation anxiety, not being house trained, aggression or nervousness. Helping a rescued dog to settle and overcome behavioural problems is mostly a matter of common sense – but if you feel out of your depth, do not delay in seeking expert advice.

Rescued dogs are often a challenge, but very rewarding when they get over their hang-ups. Training again plays a part,

and enrolling on a basic obedience course, attending ringcraft or even agility classes can often help a dog overcome his fears and build a bond between you. It may take some time – sometimes up to a year – before your rescued dog becomes a settled and integral member of the family, but it is worth being patient. You are taking on a big commitment, but a German Shepherd deserves a second chance.

THE BEST OF CARE

Chapter 5

In this chapter we will look at the needs of a German Shepherd Dog both nutritionally and in terms of general care, encompassing the mental and physical requirements of the breed. We will look at the changing needs from puppyhood right through to caring for the veteran dog.

NUTRITION

This subject could take up the whole book in itself, as there is a myriad of diets and beliefs relating to a dog's nutritional requirements. Some are based on fact and science, and others are based on opinion, but, at the end of the day, we should always be looking to keep our dogs as healthy as possible – after all, you only get out what you put in. If you feed the cheapest food, don't expect good results; conversely, if you splash out on a tailormade food of the highest quality, then expect to pay a good price.

TYPES OF DIET

Years ago we fed our dogs scraps to keep them alive, and most dogs were invariably underweight and malnourished. We then moved on to tinned foods, and then complete dry diets that were designed to give a balanced diet to the dog, containing all the basic essential nutrients. These diets are more convenient, but don't necessarily keep your dog in the best condition. They often constitute a cheaper alternative, based on the basic requirements of a dog. We then graduated to premium and super premium foods that are tailormade to suit an individual dog's needs, based on age, size and body condition. There are light diets for overweight dogs, diets for the mature animal, diets for pregnant and nursing bitches – the list is endless. You can even get diets specifically for an individual breed, and the German Shepherd is well represented in this field. These highly specialised diets look at the unique issues that surround the breed.

Currently, natural diets, such as BARF (Biologically Appropriate Raw Food) are finding favour. This type of diet is based on a natural approach to feeding dogs, which requires the owner to gain a wide-ranging knowledge of nutrition, plus the ability to spot the changes in a dog's condition and to adjust the diet accordingly. In principle, this theory is a sound one if you have the time and expertise to ensure that your dog is receiving his full nutritional needs.

As you can see, the choice of diets is endless, but, as a rule of thumb, I would always feed a fully balanced diet specifically for the breed.

Tinned food is fed with a mixer biscuit.

There is increasing interest in providing a more natural diet.

A complete diet is manufactured to meet all your dog's nutritional needs.

PUPPY FEEDING

It is imperative when feeding a German Shepherd puppy to follow the guidelines set out by the breeder. Hopefully, the breeder has reared the puppy to the condition where he has a good body shape without being too fat or too thin; the pup should have good bone and a healthy coat. If you play around with diets at this stage, it can be to the detriment of the growing puppy.

Most quality puppy foods are based on a ratio of around 30 per cent protein level, with 13-14 per cent fat, and 30-32 per cent carbohydrate. The important factor is for steady growth, so a calcium/phosphorus ratio of around 1:1 is essential. If you are feeding a complete or premium puppy food, do not supplement the diet, as this can be potentially dangerous. In fact, the majority of growth issues are the result of owners interfering with the diet.

CHANGING DIET

If you choose to change the diet at any time, it should be firstly for legitimate reasons, such as problems with availability or issues affecting your puppy's health – do not just change for change's sake.

Any change of diet should be gradually introduced. The guideline is:

Day 1 & 2: $1/4$ new diet to $3/4$ old
Day 3 & 4: $1/2$ & $1/2$
Day 5 & 6: $3/4$ new to $1/4$ old
Day 7 – 100 per cent new diet

This regime will almost guarantee a steady transition with the minimal amount of disruption to the digestive system.

If you give treats as a training aid, I always recommend using part of the daily ration rather than introducing new types of food. Excess quantities of fatty or sugary treats can, in some cases, cause digestive upset.

HEALTH ISSUES

The German Shepherd has a number of preventable health issues that, with the correct nutrition, can be avoided or limited.

DIGESTIVE PROBLEMS

German Shepherds are prone to digestive upset; they don't take to sudden changes in diet, and may have a tendency towards soft/runny stools. Therefore, a diet that is highly digestible with a quality source of ingredients is essential. The following ratio is recommended:

- Protein: 23-25 per cent
- Fats (which contain sources of Omega 3 and 6): 18-20 per cent
- Carbohydrate: 30-32 per cent

The diet also needs a good fibre content to ease the digestive transit through the system, and finally a good balance of vitamins and minerals.

You also need to keep a check on the quantity of stools that are passed. If you are feeding a diet whereby a pound of food is going in one end and nearly a pound of food is coming out of the other end, you can be sure that not much is going on in between and you are therefore unlikely to see a healthy dog with a glossy coat and a healthy digestive system. If you are concerned about your dog's diet, ask your vet for advice.

ARTHRITIC PROBLEMS

The German Shepherd is an active breed and is prone to

HUNGER STRIKE

When you get your new puppy it is quite normal for him to go off his food for a few days. This is generally due to the sudden change in surroundings and the fact that the puppy is getting a lot more attention. This, coupled with the absence of competition from littermates, means that food can be the last thought on his mind. To help your pup focus on his food, feed him away from distractions.

The worst mistake you can make is to change the food as your puppy is settling into his new home, as this will often cause diarrhoea. It may also encourage your pup to become fussy, as he will naturally think that he will get something else if he refuses the diet.

Another point to bear in mind is not to get too stressed if your puppy is not eating, as he will pick up on this and may associate the feeding ritual as an unpleasant experience and avoid food when you are around. As long as there is fresh water available, your puppy will be fine. If the fasting period extends beyond four days, I would seek veterinary advice, but as long as the puppy seems bright and shows no sign of sickness or diarrhoea, it is quite normal to go one or two days without eating.

Do not change your puppy's diet when he is settling into his new home.

It is your job to find a diet that suits your German Shepherd, taking account of any special needs if necessary.

arthritic problems. It has been found that a food containing good levels of glucosamine and chondroitin, or given as a supplement, can be helpful.

TORSION
One of the biggest problems with large breeds is GDV (gastric dilatation volvulus) or torsion. This condition can be fatal if it is not treated immediately. As preventative measures, we can assist by not exercising dogs two hours before and after feeding, and by reducing the rate at which the food is ingested. Some dogs are like vacuum cleaners and clear their food in seconds. To slow down ingestion, the food can be served soaked, and some bespoke dry foods have specifically designed kibble shapes to encourage the dog to chew.

THE OLDER SHEPHERD
With the older dog it is important not to overload the stomach, so feed little and often. There are a lot of diets specifically tailored to suit the veteran or senior dog. This type of diet will usually have:

- Reduced levels of phosphorus to aid the renal function
- Slightly higher levels of protein and essential vitamins to prevent muscle wastage
- Additives such as taurine (found in beef), which aid cardiac function.

When feeding an older dog, give everything in moderation.

GOLDEN RULE

Feed the adult dog twice daily, always ensuring that there is plenty of fresh water available – this is essential when feeding a dry diet.

Nutritional needs will change as a dog grows older.

Do not overdo the treats, as there is a tendency for the older, more sedentary dog to become overweight. A Shepherd that is getting on in years may not be able to cope with a lot of exercise, and it is all too easy to indulge your old friend by giving him extra treats. But you have to bear in mind that you can, unintentionally, curtail your dog's life by killing him with kindness.

EXERCISING YOUR SHEPHERD

When we look at the German Shepherd and its origins, we see a herding dog that is capable of working for long periods at a time. But some of us forget that the breed also needs periods of rest, which is equally important for recovery. There is a purist school of thought that suggests prolonged periods of exercise are required for the breed, but unless you are using a Shepherd for the purpose it was originally bred for, this is quite ridiculous. Equally, it should be emphasised that the Shepherd is not a couch potato, nor should he be allowed to become one.

When we look at an exercise regime for a German Shepherd, we should consider both the quality and the duration of the exercise period.

QUALITY OF EXERCISE

With regard to quality, regular exercise is a must; fair-weather walkers should not have a large and demanding breed. The climate in the UK does not assist in fair-weather exercise, so buy yourself some good waterproof clothing and get out every day, rain or shine. The odd day's missed walk will not do any harm, but we should consider

EXERCISING A GERMAN SHEPHERD

The German Shepherd is built for endurance and will thrive
on as much exercise as you can provide.

that exercise has psychological benefits on an animal (and on us), so long periods of inactivity can affect the dog both mentally and physically.

We should also look at the effectiveness of both lead walking and free-running. Lead walking or road work can develop certain muscle groups and is obviously good for a dog, but if this is combined with periods of free-running, it will give the dog a good all-round work out. Before you introduce free-running, you must be confident that your dog will return to you on command (see Chapter Six: Training and Socialisation). Free-running should only be undertaken in safe areas, without livestock and certainly not by the roadside; it is imperative that we are responsible and always abide by local open space regulations and the country code.

DURATION OF EXERCISE
Depending on the age and condition of the dog, I recommend one hour of free-running exercise per day, or one-and-a-half hours of lead walking

for an adult dog over 12 months. You may think that if you have a reasonably sized garden, that this will suffice, but this is not the case. If you observe your dog, you will see that for much of the time he spends in the garden, he is either mooching around or lying down and watching the world go by, neither of which are conducive to fitness.

PUPPY EXERCISE

A puppy's exercise regime is extremely important, as so much damage can occur at this vital growth phase. The German Shepherd does not finish growing until he is around 15 months of age; some schools of thought say that the bones do not fully ossify until two years. However, it is important that a careful exercise regime is strictly observed to ensure steady, unhindered growth.

If you observe your puppy, you will see that he spends a long time sleeping followed by short bursts of play. It is essential that you let this happen unhindered, as play and sleep are of equal importance. In the early stages of puppyhood, up to 12 weeks, the play periods can be used for basic training sessions, getting your pup used to the lead and coming when called. I take my puppies to my front gate on a lead and get them used to the cars going up and down the road before even venturing out.

After the vaccination period I then start basic exercise of approximately 100 yards and no more. I take the pups to training

Exercise must be limited during the vulnerable growing stage.

PROPER USE OF CRATES

Some experts advocate crating a puppy for prolonged periods of time, but I believe this is cruel and should be avoided. The only time I would crate a dog of this size would be if he were convalescing after an operation, when there are other dogs around, or when travelling in a vehicle for his own protection. If you intend leaving a puppy for long periods of time while you go to work, I would seriously reconsider your choice of breed, as a German Shepherd puppy is certainly not suitable – the dog's welfare must always be paramount.

A MENTAL CHALLENGE
Remember that keeping your Shepherd's mind occupied is just as important as physical exercise.

classes once a week, but I don't start proper exercise until they are six months old. At this point, I slowly build up exercise by a few yards per day until they are doing about one hour at 12 months. Some breeders recommend no exercise at all in the formative months. I personally disagree with this, as there is a great deal of evidence that inactivity is equally as bad for the puppy, resulting in lack of bone density and strength.

EXERCISING THE OLDER DOG
With the older dog, regular exercise should still be maintained albeit over much shorter distances. It is sad to see an old dog limping down the road, loyally following his master. However, it is equally sad to see activity suddenly halted by the owner just because the dog has reached a landmark in age.

I have a 12-year-old Shepherd who has the activity level of a five-year-old, but I have had younger dogs who could only manage shorter distances due to arthritis. The most important consideration is to gauge exercise to suit an individual dog's needs. Sometimes a vet will recommend that the exercise regime is maintained in an old dog with musculo-skeletal problems, but is reduced to short walks to aid mobility.

MENTAL STIMULATION
When we are discussing exercise, we should also consider the psychological aspects. I have had many conversations with owners who have young dogs, complaining that their dog has too much energy or, in the owner's opinion, is hyperactive. The use of this word invariably tells me that the dog lacks mental stimulation. Prolonged exercise as a solution for a dog who has too much energy merely results in a very fit, hyperactive dog.

The classic case is a young male who is driving his owners crazy, as he never seems to settle down, even after prolonged periods of exercise. There are two

Agility training provides the opportunity for your Shepherd to exercise his mind and his body.

things to consider: firstly and most obviously, the German Shepherd is an active dog; secondly, he is an intelligent animal. If the average person was sat in a room for hours on end with no mental stimulation whatsoever, I am sure they would be climbing the walls in frustration. The situation is worse in a young dog who is constantly looking for stimulation in varying degrees from normal inquisitiveness to manic behavioural traits and hyperactivity. So how do we control this and have a calming effect?

Play is one activity that certainly helps. However, this should not be confined to playing chase the ball. Take it one step further and hide the ball, or a favourite toy, so the dog has to use his nose. Start hiding the ball nearby, and then slowly increase the distance, making it gradually harder. This is the basis of all nose work, and when you see a dog who has been working for maybe 10 or 15 minutes, you would find it difficult to differentiate it from a dog who has had a lot of exercise.

Consider this: if I laid a fine strand of cotton thread along the ground for maybe 20 metres and asked you to follow it using only your eyes, your faculties would be seriously tested, resulting in a feeling of tiredness. Like you, a dog uses all his concentration to follow the trail, the only difference being that the dog would use his nose. Another parallel would be if you did a day's hard, manual labour; you would be physically tired, but still quite mentally active. Conversely, if you did a day in the office, poring over figures, accounts and the like, I know from experience that you would be physically and mentally tired, as it is a proven fact that the brain goes into recovery mode after long periods of mental exercise. If you are not sure of this analogy, try reading a difficult book and staying awake…

The hyperactive dog, more often than not, is just lacking mental stimulation. There is a saying that 'the devil makes work for idle hands'; he certainly does, often seen when your dog destroys something dear to you. So, in conclusion, exercise is about quality and quantity and should never be excessive or non-existent.

COAT CARE

The German Shepherd is not a heavy-coated breed that requires long periods of grooming, as an Afghan Hound or Old English Sheepdog does; neither does he have a close, short coat like a Whippet or Dobermann, which is very easy to keep in order. The German Shepherd has a coat that requires a regular maintenance regime. Like most breeds, the German Shepherd has a double coat made up of a dense undercoat and a harsh-textured top coat. In some Shepherds, the top coat can be quite heavy and requires quite a lot of care.

PUPPY GROOMING

As always, it is best to get your dog used to being handled from a very young age so that he learns to accept a grooming routine.

I start with a large, wire slicker brush, using a steady stroking motion from the head

to the tail. Initially, I try not to dig too deeply into the coat, but once the puppy is used to being groomed, I progressively work the brush deeper into the coat. You may find that the puppy struggles to begin with, but if you pick the right time, such as when he's a bit sleepy, you will find it easier, and the puppy will find it therapeutic, making the grooming ritual easily acceptable for him.

It is important to groom little and often in these early days, as overdoing it may result in the pup becoming restless and irritable. Whatever you do, don't turn it into a wrestling match with the pup, as you will always end up having a battle of wills whenever you try any kind of grooming.

When your puppy starts to

ANAL GLANDS

An overlooked area that requires care is the dog's anus. German Shepherds are prone to anal gland infections where the anus becomes inflamed. If this happens, the anal glands will need to be emptied by your vet. In more severe cases a Shepherd can suffer from anal furunculosis, which is a condition where lesions are found around the anus. This condition requires immediate veterinary attention. So although checking the anus is not the most pleasant aspect of your care regime, it should not be overlooked. For more information, see Chapter Eight: Happy and Healthy.

accept the brush with ease, then, and only then, should you introduce a comb. The best type is a metal comb with the teeth approximately 2 mm apart. Again, don't be too overzealous at the start. If this type of grooming ritual is done every day, it is surprising what results you can achieve.

ADULT GROOMING

If you accustom your puppy to being groomed, he will positively enjoy his grooming sessions in adulthood; my older Shepherds really enjoy it when the comb comes out. Regular grooming is essential for an adult dog; a minimum of two sessions per week is needed to maintain a healthy coat, removing all the dead hairs and encouraging new growth.

After you have finished combing and brushing, wipe over the dog with a piece of velvet or corduroy to take out any small dust particles and stray hairs. This gives a shiny finish to the coat, especially if your Shepherd has a black saddle.

The coat normally moults about twice a year; in bitches this is often around the time of their season. If you groom regularly, it avoids large amounts of hair being shed in one go and prevents those unsightly tufts on the dog's loins and feathering around the thighs.

PUPPY CARE

Accustom your puppy to being handled so that he is happy
to be groomed and examined by a vet, if necessary.

Brush your puppy, using gentle strokes.

Check the ears to make sure they are clean and fresh-smelling.

Lift each paw in turn and check the nails and the pads.

Teach your puppy to have his teeth examined – and then reward him with a treat.

With older dogs it is important not to be too vigorous, and to be aware of lumps and bumps. A regular grooming ritual maintains a good bond and keeps you in tune with your dog's health. When I judge dogs, I often find a lump or cyst that the owner was oblivious to. But if you keep in touch with your dog's coat and skin, you can spot signs of change and identify early symptoms of cysts, warts, ticks and fleas and malignant lumps that can receive prompt treatment.

BATHTIME
Bathing should be performed about every six months or when the coat is really dirty, and not on puppies under six months. If you bathe your dog too frequently, you strip out all the natural oils in the coat, which act as a barrier to protect the skin.

When bathing your Shepherd use a good-quality shampoo, not a human shampoo – and certainly not washing up liquid – as both can have a detrimental effect on the dog's skin. I recommend a good herbal shampoo, such as tea tree oil, which is a natural insecticide.

Pick a warm day so your Shepherd does not get too cold when he is drying off. A good tip is to groom your dog before you bathe him; this assists in separating the hairs to aid thorough shampooing.

- Soak the coat thoroughly with warm water, avoiding the eyes and ears.
- Mix up the required amount of shampoo in an empty plastic bottle with warm water. You will need about 1 part shampoo to 10 parts water.
- Apply the shampoo over the coat, massaging well into the skin. Do not forget the tail and undercarriage.
- Rinse the shampoo out thoroughly. If the dog's coat is really dirty, a second application may be required; but normally, with a good-quality shampoo, once should suffice.
- When thoroughly rinsed, let the dog have a good shake and then towel dry to remove as much excess water as possible.
- Leave your dog to dry, or use a hair-dryer and then groom again. If you choose a winter's day, ensure your dog is dried thoroughly to prevent him from getting a chill.

TEETH
Teeth are difficult to maintain and are often neglected, as owners tend to think that, by the mere action of eating, the teeth will clean themselves. There are many products available from toothpastes to dental bars, all designed to promote healthy teeth and gums. Before we explore the best practice for ensuring white, healthy teeth, it is helpful to understand how teeth can deteriorate and the detrimental effects of poor oral hygiene.

A longcoated German Shepherd will need regular grooming to keep his coat free of mats and tangles.

During a normal daily feeding regime, bacteria and calcium (tartar) form on the tooth. Slowly, more and more bacteria form into plaque, which builds and thickens within days. The underlying bacteria are starved of oxygen and therefore begin to populate the gums. In the long-term the gums become severely affected, resulting in tissue loss and bone destruction. The prolonged untreated state can result in long-term periodontal disease that can affect the kidneys and liver, and, in extreme cases, the brain. Hopefully, long before a dog gets into this state, veterinary advice would be sought, resulting in a full descale and polish.

Most modern dry diets contain calcium chelators, such as sodium polyphosphate, which is often found in toothpaste. These prevent the accumulation of calcium, which is the building block for tartar, and when combined with the mechanical brushing action caused by crunching on the kibble, can seriously reduce tartar formation.

Oral chewing bars have the same effect, but nothing can replace daily brushing, if your dog is happy to let you do it. There are some very good toothpastes on the market that have many different tastes to tempt your dog.

If your dog will not accept teeth cleaning, I would suggest a good-quality smoked bone, which doesn't splinter easily. I don't normally recommend marrowbones, as they can cause

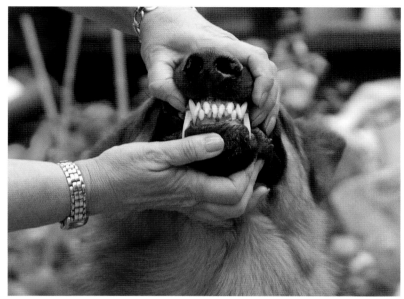

If necessary, teeth should be brushed to prevent the build-up of tartar.

DENTAL EXAMINATION

Try to get into the habit of examining your dog's mouth and teeth on a regular basis. Again, start this at the puppy stage so your Shepherd gets used to being handled in this way.

- Gently place one hand under the lower jaw and stroke the head from the tip of the nose backward.
- When your puppy is relaxed in the above position, raise the lips – don't squeeze – a little at a time.
- Work on this handling procedure for a few days, and your Shepherd will be happy to let you examine his mouth and teeth.

Never place your hand over the nostrils, as this will upset your Shepherd, making it harder to look at the mouth. Be careful, especially if you have long nails, and don't try this exercise if your puppy's gums are red and swollen. This indicates that he is teething, and he won't appreciate being messed with at this time.

Make sure your puppy has plenty of chew toys when he is teething.

is to take off a small amount, say a couple of millimetres at a time, on a regularly trimmed nail. To be on the safe side, buy styptic powder or liquid from your vet or a good pet shop, which quickly stems the flow of blood if you ever catch the quick.

As in all aspects of handling your Shepherd, it is important that you start trimming nails from an early age. The breeder will have kept the puppies' nails in trim, so they will have some knowledge of the procedure. I normally use a pair of human nail trimmers, as they are easy to use on a small puppy. If you observe your puppy's nails, you will see the new growth as lighter and semi-transparent and often with a slight hook at the tip. I use this hook as a gauge of how much to take off.

digestive upset. Never leave your dog unattended with a bone for prolonged periods of time, as he could swallow small shards or splinters. If the bone starts to deteriorate in this way, throw it in the bin.

TEETHING TIP
If your puppy is teething and chewing a lot, try giving him an old hand towel. A puppy can sink his teeth into the towel quite easily, with a bit of pressure, and this helps to remove the loose teeth – and it also saves the furniture from being ruined.

NAILS
A dog's nails can grow at varying speeds, but it is essential that

they are not allowed to get too long. In most cases, a regular ritual of nail trimming is needed to keep the feet tidy and healthy. Nail clippers can be either the guillotine type or the cutter plier type; make sure they are kept sharp and in good condition. If you wish, you can finish off with a nail file, but quite often this is not needed.

Most people are terrified of cutting their dog's nails, as they are worried about cutting through the quick, the blood vessel that makes up the core of the nail. This is understandable, as, when the quick is cut, it seems to bleed for a long time. The best plan

If your German Shepherd is used to having his nails trimmed from an early age, he will not resent the procedure.

If you have taken the time to get your puppy used to being handled without turning it into a wrestling match, you will find nail trimming relatively easy. If your puppy objects, I would suggest taking time to handle his feet on a daily basis. The same applies to handling the legs, body, face and ears: the more frequently you do it, the less of a battle you will have later on.

If you are worried about cutting your puppy's nails, seek the professional services from a vet or a groomer, or an experienced dog owner may be able to help.

EARS
The ears should be kept clean, and should normally be a faded pink colour. Any waxy or dirt build-up should be removed by using ear wipes, or a wad of cotton wool with a drop of surgical spirit on it. Gently work from the inside to the tip of the ear. Don't over-soak the cotton wool, as you don't want liquid dripping into the ear. Under no circumstances should you use cotton buds to remove build-up from the inner ear; you can do more harm than good by pushing debris back down the ear canal.

If your dog has a dirty build-up deep into the ear, you can purchase a proprietary liquid ear cleaner, which dissolves earwax build-up, leaving the ear clean. If there are signs of infection, a reddening of the inner ear, and the dog is scratching his ears and shaking his head, then you should seek veterinary advice.

A well-cared-for German Shepherd is full of energy and is the picture of good health.

EYES
As long as the eyes are bright and there is no film across them, they are healthy. The everyday dirt and dust that gathers in the corner of the eye can be removed by using a cotton wool bud or soft tissue. Simply wipe the build-up from the corner of the eye, away from the eye in the direction of the nose, ensuring that it is completely removed. An old remedy is to use cold tea, no milk or sugar, as a salve for the eye to keep it healthy and fight against infection. Proprietary eye drops can be used to the same effect. If there is any sign of long term or heavy build-up of matter, seek veterinary advice.

SUMMING UP
In conclusion, your German Shepherd should be healthy and vibrant with the mental and physical alertness associated with a working dog. Keeping your dog in the peak of health and vitality is no easy feat, but it can be attained by the quality and regularity of a care regime.

Good feeding, exercise, grooming and general care are a must. If you buy an expensive car, you regularly service it, you fill it with the right oil, and you keep it clean and polished. The same principles apply to caring for your dog: if you feed the cheapest food, only take him out once in a while, let him get dirty and don't take care of him, he will not thrive. You could give some people the Crown Jewels to look after and they would be returned tarnished; I trust that you, dear reader, are not one of those people…

TRAINING AND SOCIALISATION

Chapter 6

When you decided to bring a German Shepherd Dog into your life, you probably had dreams of how it was going to be: long walks together, cosy evenings with a Shepherd lying devotedly at your feet, and whenever you returned home, there would always be a special welcome waiting for you.

There is no doubt that you can achieve all this – and much more – with a Shepherd, but like anything that is worth having, you must be prepared to put in the work. A German Shepherd, regardless of whether it is a puppy or an adult, does not come ready trained, understanding exactly what you want and fitting perfectly into your lifestyle. A Shepherd has to learn his place in your family and he must discover what is acceptable behaviour.

We have a great starting point in that the German Shepherd has an outstanding temperament. The breed was developed to be a loyal and biddable companion, with the instincts to herd and protect livestock. The Shepherds of today retain these instincts, but what is paramount is their desire to work under direction. The German Shepherd is a highly intelligent dog, and it is up to you, the owner, to channel his energies to produce a well-trained, well-behaved companion that will be a pleasure to own.

THE FAMILY PACK
Dogs have been domesticated for some 14,000 years, but, luckily for us, they have inherited and retained behaviour from their distant ancestor – the wolf. A German Shepherd may never have lived in the wild, but he is born with the survival skills and the mentality of a meat-eating predator who hunts in a pack. A wolf living in a pack owes its existence to mutual co-operation and an acceptance of a hierarchy, as this ensures both food and protection. A domesticated dog living in a family pack has exactly the same outlook. He wants food, companionship, and leadership – and it is your job to provide for these needs.

YOUR ROLE
Theories about dog behaviour and methods of training go in and out of fashion, but in reality, nothing has changed from the day when wolves ventured in from the wild to join the family circle. The wolf (and equally the dog) accepts a subservient place in the family pack in return for food and protection. In a dog's eyes, you are his leader, and he relies on you to make all the important decisions. This does not mean that you have to act like a dictator or a bully. You are accepted as a

Do you have what it takes to be a firm, fair and consistent leader?

leader, without argument, as long as you have the right credentials.

The first part of the job is easy. You are the provider, and you are therefore respected because you supply food. In a German Shepherd's eyes, you must be the ultimate hunter because a day never goes by when you cannot find food. The second part of the leader's job description is straightforward, but for some reason we find it hard to achieve. In order for a dog to accept his place in the family pack he must respect his leader as the decision-maker. A low-ranking pack animal does not question authority; he is perfectly happy to see someone else shoulder the responsibility. Problems will only arise if you cut a poor figure as leader and the dog feels he should mount a challenge for the top-ranking role.

HOW TO BE A GOOD LEADER

There are a number of guidelines to follow to establish yourself in the role of leader in a way that your German Shepherd understands and respects. If you have a puppy, you may think you don't have to take this on board for a few months, but that would be a big mistake. Start as you mean to go on, and your pup will be quick to find his place in his new family.

- **Keep it simple:** Decide on the rules you want your German Shepherd to obey and always make it 100 per cent clear what is acceptable, and what is unacceptable, behaviour.
- **Be consistent:** If you are not consistent about enforcing rules, how can you expect your German Shepherd to take you seriously? There is nothing worse than allowing your Shepherd to jump up at you one moment and then scolding him the next time he does it because you were wearing your best clothes. As far as the German Shepherd is concerned, he may as well try it on because he can't predict your reaction.

- **Get your timing right:** If you are rewarding your German Shepherd, and equally if you are reprimanding him, you must respond within one to two seconds otherwise the dog will not link his behaviour with your reaction (see page 86).
- **Read your dog's body language:** Find out how to read body language and facial expressions (see page 85) so that you understand your Shepherd's feelings and his intentions.
- **Be aware of your own body language:** When you ask your German Shepherd to do something, do not bend over him and talk to him at eye level. Assert your authority by standing over him and keeping an upright posture. Obviously, if you have a timid dog, you would not seek to make him more fearful by doing this. You can also help your dog to learn by using your body language to communicate with him. For example, if you want your dog to come to you, open your arms out and look inviting. If you want your dog to stay, use a hand signal (palm flat, facing the dog) so you are effectively 'blocking' his advance.
- **Tone of voice:** German Shepherds are very receptive to tone of voice, so you can use your voice to praise him or to correct undesirable behaviour. If you are pleased with your Shepherd, praise him to the skies in a warm, happy voice. If you want to stop him raiding the bin, use a deep, stern voice

A dog will pay far more attention to body language than to verbal communication.

If you understand your dog's body language, you can anticipate his intentions. This adult German Shepherd is giving out friendly vibes to a young puppy.

when you say "No".

- **Give one command only:** If you keep repeating a command, or keep changing it, your German Shepherd will think you are babbling and will probably ignore you. If your Shepherd does not respond the first time you ask, make it simple by using a treat to lure him into position, and then you can reward him for a correct response.
- **Daily reminders:** A young, exuberant Shepherd is apt to forget his manners from time to time, and an adolescent dog may attempt to challenge your authority (see page 98). Rather than coming down on your

German Shepherd like a ton of bricks when he does something wrong, try to prevent bad manners by daily reminders of good manners. For example:

- i   Do not let your dog barge ahead of you when you are going through a door.
- ii Do not let him leap out of the car the moment you open the door (which could be potentially lethal, as well as being disrespectful).
- iii Do not let him eat from your hand when you are at the table.
- iv Do not let him 'win' a toy at the end of a play session and then make off with it.

You 'own' his toys, and you must end every play session on your terms.

UNDERSTANDING YOUR GERMAN SHEPHERD

Body language is an important means of communication between dogs, which they use to make friends, to assert status, and to avoid conflict. It is important to get on your dog's wavelength by understanding his body language and reading his facial expressions.

- A positive body posture and a wagging tail indicate a happy, confident dog.
- A crouched body posture with ears back and tail down show that a dog is being submissive.

A dog may do this when he is being told off or if a more assertive dog approaches him.

- A bold dog will stand tall, looking strong and alert. His ears will be forward and his tail will be held high.
- A dog who raises his hackles (lifting the fur along his topline) is trying to look as scary as possible. This may be the prelude to aggressive behaviour, but, in many cases, the dog is apprehensive and is unsure how to cope with a situation.
- A playful dog will go down on his front legs while standing on his hind legs in a bow position. This friendly invitation says: "I'm no threat, let's play."
- A dominant, aggressive dog will meet other dogs with a hard stare. If he is challenged, he may bare his teeth and growl, and the corners of his mouth will be drawn forward. His ears will be forward and he will appear tense in every muscle (see pages 103 and 105).
- A nervous dog will often show aggressive behaviour as a means of self-protection. If threatened, this dog will lower his head and flatten his ears. The corners of his mouth may be drawn back, and he may bark or whine.

GIVING REWARDS

Why should your German Shepherd do as you ask? If you follow the guidelines given above, your Shepherd should respect your authority, but what about the time when he is playing with a new doggy friend or has found a really enticing scent? The answer is that you must always be the most interesting, the most attractive, and the most irresistible person in your Shepherd's eyes. It would be nice to think you could achieve this by personality alone, but most of us need a little extra help. You need to find out what is the biggest treat you can give your dog – it may be food or it may be a game with a favourite toy – and to give him this reward when he does as you ask. Some Shepherds work for food, but most prefer to be rewarded with a toy. Remember, you must always remain in charge of the toy, initiating play sessions, and deciding when to end the game. In this way, you rise in your Shepherd's estimation, as you are in charge of something that he really wants.

When you are teaching a dog a new exercise, you should reward him frequently. When he knows the exercise or command, reward him randomly so that he keeps on responding to you in a positive manner. If your dog does something extra special, like leaving his canine chum mid-play in the park, make sure he really knows how pleased you are by giving him a handful of treats or throwing his ball a few extra times. If he gets a bonanza reward, he is more likely to come back on future occasions, because you have proved to be even more rewarding than his previous activity.

TOP TREATS

Some trainers grade treats depending on what they are

Find out what works as a reward when you are training – this Shepherd prefers a game with a toy to a food treat.

asking the dog to do. A dog may get a low-grade treat, such as a piece of dry food, to reward good behaviour on a random basis, such as sitting when you open a door or allowing you to examine his teeth. But a high-grade treat, such as cooked liver, is reserved for training new exercises or for use in the park when you want a really good recall. Whatever type of treat you use, remember to subtract it from your Shepherd's daily ration. Fat Shepherds are lethargic, prone to health problems, and will almost certainly have a shorter life expectancy. Reward your Shepherd, but always keep a check on his figure!

HOW DO DOGS LEARN?

It is not difficult to get inside your German Shepherd's head and understand how he learns, as it is not dissimilar to the way we learn. Dogs learn by conditioning: they find out that specific behaviours produce specific consequences. This is known as operant conditioning or consequence learning. Consequences have to be immediate or clearly linked to the behaviour, as a dog sees the world in terms of action and result. Dogs will quickly learn if an action has a bad consequence or a good consequence.

Dogs also learn by association. This is known as classical conditioning or association learning. It is the type of learning made famous by Pavlov's experiment with dogs. Pavlov presented dogs with food and measured their salivary response

If you are using food treats, make sure they are bite-size and easy to swallow.

(how much they drooled). Then he rang a bell just before presenting the food. At first, the dogs did not salivate until the food was presented. But after a while they learnt that the sound of the bell meant that food was coming, and so they salivated when they heard the bell. A dog needs to learn the association in order for it to have any meaning. For example, a dog that has never seen a lead before will be completely indifferent to it. A dog that has learnt that a lead means he is going for a walk will get excited the second he sees the lead; he has learnt to associate a lead with a walk.

BE POSITIVE

The most effective method of training dogs is to use their ability to learn by consequence and to teach that the behaviour you want produces a good consequence. For example, if you ask your German Shepherd to "Sit", and reward him with his toy, he will learn that it is worth his while to sit on command because it will lead to a game. He is far more likely to repeat the behaviour, and the behaviour will become stronger, because it results in a positive outcome. This method of training is known as positive reinforcement, and it generally leads to a happy, co-operative dog

THE CLICKER REVOLUTION

Karen Pryor pioneered the technique of clicker training when she was working with dolphins. It is very much a continuation of Pavlov's work and makes full use of association learning.

Karen wanted to mark 'correct' behaviour at the precise moment it happened. She found it was impossible to toss a fish to a dolphin when it was in mid-air, when she wanted to reward it. Her aim was to establish a conditioned response so the dolphin knew that it had performed correctly and a reward would follow.

The solution was the clicker: a small matchbox-shaped training aid, with a metal tongue that makes a click when it is pressed. To begin with, the dolphin had to learn that a click meant that food was coming. The dolphin then learnt that it

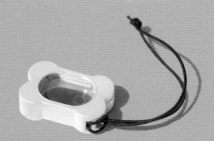

must 'earn' a click in order to get a reward. Clicker training has been used with many different animals, most particularly with dogs, and it has proved hugely successful. It is a great aid for pet owners and is also widely used by professional trainers who teach highly specialised skills.

that is willing to work, and a handler who has fun training their dog.

The opposite approach is negative reinforcement. This is far less effective and often results in a poor relationship between dog and owner. In this method of training, you ask your German Shepherd to "Sit", and, if he does not respond, you deliver a sharp yank on the training collar or push his rear to the ground. The dog learns that not responding to your command has a bad consequence, and he may be less likely to ignore you in the future. However, it may well have a bad consequence for

you, too. A dog that is treated in this way may associate harsh handling with the handler and become aggressive or fearful. Instead of establishing a pattern of willing co-operation, you are establishing a relationship built on coercion.

GETTING STARTED

As you train your German Shepherd, you will develop your own techniques as you get to know what motivates him. You may decide to get involved with clicker training or you may prefer to go for a simple command-and-reward formula. It does not matter

what form of training you use, as long as it is based on positive, reward-based methods.

There are a few important guidelines to bear in mind when you are training your Shepherd:

- Find a training area that is free from distractions, particularly when you are just starting out.
- Keep training sessions short, especially with young puppies that have very short attention spans.
- Do not train if you are in a bad mood or if you are on a tight schedule – the training session will be doomed to failure.

- If you are using a toy as a reward, make sure it is only available when you are training. In this way it has an added value for your Shepherd.
- If you are using food treats, make sure they are bite-size and easy to swallow; you don't want to hang about while your Shepherd chews on his treat.
- All food treats must be deducted from your Shepherd's daily food ration.
- When you are training, move around your allocated area so that your dog does not think that an exercise can only be performed in one place.
- If your German Shepherd Dog is finding an exercise difficult, try not to become frustrated. Go back a step and praise him for his effort. You will probably find he is more successful when you try again at the next training session.
- Always end training sessions on a happy, positive note. Ask your Shepherd to do something you know he can do – it could be a trick he enjoys performing – and then reward him with a few treats or an extra-long play session.

In the exercises that follow, clicker training is introduced and followed, but all the exercises will work without the use of a clicker.

It does not take long for a dog to realise that he must 'earn' a click to get a reward

INTRODUCING A CLICKER
The intelligent German Shepherd will quickly learn what the clicker means. Introductory training can be combined with attention training, which is a very useful tool and can be used on many different occasions. At this stage, you can decide whether your Shepherd prefers to work for food treats or for a toy.

- Prepare some treats or select a suitable toy, and go to an area that is free from distractions. When your German Shepherd stops sniffing around and looks at you, click and reward by throwing him a treat or his toy. This means he will not crowd you, but will go looking for the reward. Repeat a couple of times. If your Shepherd is very easily distracted, you may need to start this exercise with the dog on a lead.
- After a few clicks, your German Shepherd will understand that if he hears a click, he will get a reward. He must now learn that he must 'earn' a click. This time, when your German Shepherd looks at you, wait a little longer before clicking, and then reward him. If your Shepherd is on a lead but responding well, try him off the lead.
- When your German Shepherd Dog is reliably working for a click and giving you his full attention, you can introduce a cue or command word, such as "Watch". Repeat the exercise a few times, using the cue. You now have a German Shepherd Dog that understands the clicker and will give you his attention when you ask him to "Watch".

Hold a treat above your puppy's head, and, as he looks up, he will go into the Sit position.

Lower a treat to the ground, and your puppy will follow it, going into the Down position.

TRAINING EXERCISES

THE SIT

This is the easiest exercise to teach, so it is rewarding for both you and your German Shepherd.

- Select a treat or a toy and hold it just above your puppy's nose. As he looks up at the reward, he will naturally go into the Sit. As soon as he is in position, reward him.
- Repeat the exercise, and when your pup understands what you want, introduce the "Sit" command.
- You can practise at mealtimes by holding out the bowl and waiting for your dog to sit before placing the bowl on the floor.

THE DOWN

Work hard at this exercise because a reliable Down is useful in many different situations, and an instant Down can be a lifesaver.

- You can start with your dog in a Sit, or it is just as effective to teach it when the dog is standing. Hold a treat or a toy just below your puppy's nose, and slowly lower it towards the ground. The reward acts as a lure, and your puppy will follow it, first going down on his forequarters, and then bringing his hindquarters down as he tries to get the reward.
- Make sure you close your fist around the treat or toy, and only reward your puppy when he is in the correct position. If

your puppy is reluctant to go Down, you can apply gentle pressure on his shoulders to encourage him to go into the correct position.

- When your puppy is following the reward and going into position, introduce a verbal command.
- Build up this exercise over a period of time, each time waiting a little longer before giving the reward, so the puppy learns to stay in the Down position.

THE RECALL

It is never too soon to start training the Recall, as this is an exercise that many German Shepherd owners struggle with. Make sure you are always happy and excited when your Shepherd comes to you, even if he has been slower than you would like. He must believe that the greatest reward is coming to you.

- You can start teaching the Recall from the moment your puppy arrives home. He will naturally follow you, so keep calling his name, and reward him when he comes to you.
- Practise in the garden, and, when your puppy is busy exploring, get his attention by calling his name. As he runs towards you, introduce the verbal command "Come". Make sure you sound happy and exciting, so your puppy wants to come to you. When he responds, give him lots of praise.
- If your puppy is slow to respond, try running away a few paces, or jumping up and down. It doesn't matter how silly you look, the key issue is to get your puppy's attention and then make yourself irresistible!
- If your Shepherd goes 'deaf' on you and ignores your "Come" command, do not keep repeating it, as he will simply switch off and continue to ignore you. You need to grab his attention with a sharp "Oi", or a clap of your hands, and in the split-second he looks up at you, go on the charm offensive, changing your tone of voice to sound warm and inviting so your Shepherd wants to come to you.
- In a dog's mind, coming when

Work on getting an enthusiastic response to the Recall.

called should be regarded as the best fun because he knows he is always going to be rewarded. Never make the mistake of telling your dog off, no matter how slow he is to respond, as you will undo all your previous hard work.

- When you are free-running your dog, make sure you have his favourite toy or a pocket full of treats so you can reward him at intervals throughout the walk when you call him to you. Do not allow your dog to free-run and only call him back at the end of the walk to clip on his lead. An intelligent German

Shepherd will soon realise that the Recall means the end of his walk, and then end of fun – so who can blame him for not wanting to come back?

TRAINING LINE
This is the equivalent of a very long lead, which you can buy at a pet store, or you can make your own with a length of rope. The training line is attached to your German Shepherd's collar and should be around 15 feet (4.5 metres) in length.

The purpose of the training line is to prevent your Shepherd from disobeying you so that he never has the chance to get into bad habits. For example, when you call your Shepherd and he ignores you, you can immediately pick up the end of the training line and call him again. By picking up the line you will have attracted his attention, and if you call in an excited, happy voice, your Shepherd will come to you. The moment he comes to you, give him a tasty treat so he is instantly rewarded for making the 'right' decision.

The training line is very useful when your Shepherd becomes an adolescent and is testing your leadership. When you have reinforced the correct behaviour a number of times, your dog will build up a strong recall and you will not need to use a training line.

WALKING ON A LOOSE LEAD

This is a simple exercise, which baffles many German Shepherd owners. In most cases, owners are too impatient, wanting to get on with the expedition rather that training the dog how to walk on a lead. Take time with this one; the German Shepherd is a strong dog, and a German Shepherd that pulls on the lead is no pleasure to own. Pulling on the lead can also be a sign that a dog does not respect his owner and is trying to impose his will on proceedings. If you suspect this is the case, you will need to work on your lead training, but also work at lowering your dog's status so that he is more respectful. For more information, see Dominance, page 103.

- In the early stages of lead

training, allow your puppy to pick his route and follow him. He will get used to the feeling of being 'attached' to you, and has no reason to put up any resistance.

- Next, find a toy or a tasty treat and show it to your puppy. Let him follow the treat/toy for a few paces, and then reward him.

- Build up the amount of time your pup will walk with you, and when he is walking nicely by your side, introduce the verbal command "Heel" or "Close". Give lots of praise when your pup is in the correct position.

- When your pup is walking alongside you, keep focusing his attention on you by using his name and then rewarding

SECRET WEAPON

You can build up a strong Recall by using another form of association learning. Buy a whistle, and when you are giving your German Shepherd his food, peep on the whistle. You can choose the type of signal you want to give: two short peeps or one long whistle, for example. Within a matter of days, your dog will learn that the sound of the whistle means that food is coming.

Now transfer the lesson outside. Arm yourself with some tasty treats and the whistle. Allow your German Shepherd to run free in the garden, and, after a couple of minutes, use the whistle. The dog has already learnt to associate the whistle with

food, so he will come towards you. Immediately reward him with a treat and lots of praise. Repeat the lesson a few times in the garden so you are confident that your dog is responding before trying it in the park. Make sure you always have some treats in your pocket when you go for a walk, and your dog will quickly learn how rewarding it is to come to you.

The aim is for your Shepherd to walk on a loose lead, focusing his attention on you when required.

Build up the Stay exercise in easy stages.

him when he looks at you. If it is going well, introduce some changes of direction.

- Do not attempt to take your puppy out on the lead until you have mastered the basics at home. You need to be confident that your puppy accepts the lead and will focus his attention on you, when requested, before you face the challenge of a busy environment.
- As your German Shepherd Dog gets bigger and stronger, he may try to pull on the lead, particularly if you are heading somewhere he wants to go, such as the park. If this

happens, stop, call your dog to you, and do not set off again until he is in the correct position. You can also try changing direction without warning, as this will make your German Shepherd pay more attention to you – this works well with dogs that have learnt to pull excessively. It may take time, but your Shepherd will eventually realise that it is more productive to walk by your side than to pull ahead.

STAYS

This may not be the most exciting exercise, but it is one of the most

useful. There are many occasions when you want your German Shepherd to stay in position, even if it is only for a few seconds. The classic example is when you want your Shepherd to stay in the back of the car until you have clipped on his lead. Some trainers use the verbal command "Stay" when the dog is to remain in position for an extended period of time, and "Wait" if the dog is to stay in position for a few seconds until you give the next command. Others trainers use a universal "Stay" to cover all situations. It all comes down to personal preference, and as long as you are

From birth to seven weeks, a puppy learns by interacting with his mother and his littermates.

consistent, your dog will understand the command he is given.

- Put your puppy in a Sit or a Down. Using a hand signal (flat palm, facing the dog) to show that he is to stay in position. Step a pace away from the dog. Wait a second, step back and reward him. If you have a lively pup, you may find it easier to train this exercise on the lead.
- Repeat the exercise, gradually increasing the distance you can leave your dog. When you return to your dog's side, praise him quietly, and release him with a command, such as "OK".
- Remember to keep your body language very still when you are

training this exercise, and avoid eye contact with your dog. Work on this exercise over a period of time, and you will build up a really reliable Stay.

SOCIALISATION

While your German Shepherd is mastering basic obedience exercises, there is other, equally important, work to do with him. A German Shepherd is not only becoming a part of your home and family, he is becoming a member of the community. He needs to be able to live in the outside world, coping calmly with every new situation that comes his way. It is your job to introduce him to as many different experiences as possible and encourage him to

behave in an appropriate manner.

In order to socialise your German Shepherd effectively, it is helpful to understand how his brain is developing, and then you will get a perspective on how he sees the world.

CANINE SOCIALISATION (Birth to 7 weeks)

This is the time when a dog learns how to be a dog. By interacting with his mother and his littermates, a young pup learns about leadership and submission. He learns to read body posture so that he understands the intentions of his mother and his siblings. A puppy that is taken away from his litter too early may always have behavioural problems with other dogs, either being fearful or aggressive.

SOCIALISATION PERIOD (7 to 12 weeks)

This is the time to get cracking and introduce your Shepherd puppy to as many different experiences as possible. This includes meeting different people, other dogs and animals, seeing new sights, and hearing a range of sounds, from the vacuum cleaner to the roar of traffic. At this stage, a puppy learns very quickly and what he learns will stay with him for the rest of his life. This is the best time for a puppy to move to a new home, as he is adaptable and ready to form deep bonds.

FEAR-IMPRINT PERIOD (8 to 11 weeks)

This occurs during the socialisation period, and it can be the cause of problems if it is not handled carefully. If a pup is exposed to a frightening or painful experience, it will lead to lasting impressions. Obviously, you will attempt to avoid frightening situations, such as your pup being bullied by a mean-spirited older dog, or a firework going off, but you cannot always protect your puppy from the unexpected. If your pup has a nasty experience, the best plan is to make light of it and distract him by offering him a treat or a game. The pup will take the lead from you and will be reassured that there is nothing to worry about. If you mollycoddle him and sympathise with him, he is far more likely to retain the memory of his fear.

Start taking your puppy out to quiet places, and go to busier areas when he becomes more confident.

SENIORITY PERIOD (12 to 16 weeks)

During this period, your Shepherd puppy starts to cut the apron strings and becomes more independent. He will test out his status to find out who is the pack leader: him or you. Bad habits, such as play biting, which may have been seen as endearing a few weeks earlier, should be firmly discouraged. Remember to use positive, reward-based training, but make sure your puppy knows that you are the leader and must be respected.

SECOND FEAR-IMPRINT PERIOD (6 to 14 months)

This period is not as critical as the first fear-imprint period, but it should still be handled carefully. During this time your Shepherd may appear apprehensive or he may show fear of something familiar. You may feel as if you have taken a backwards step, but if you adopt a calm, positive manner, your Shepherd will see that there is nothing to be frightened of. Do not make your dog confront the thing that frightens him. Simply distract his attention and give him something else to think about, such as obeying a simple command, such as "Sit" or "Down". This will give you the opportunity to praise and reward your dog, and will help to boost his confidence.

Make use of every opportunity so your puppy meets and greets lots of different people.

YOUNG ADULTHOOD AND MATURITY (1 to 4 years)

The timing of this phase depends on the size of the dog: the bigger the dog, the later it is. This period coincides with a dog's increased size and strength, mental as well as physical. Some dogs, particularly those with a dominant nature, will test your leadership again and may become aggressive towards other dogs. Firmness and continued training are essential at this time so that your German Shepherd accepts his status in the family pack.

IDEAS FOR SOCIALISATION

When you are socialising your German Shepherd, you want him to experience as many different situations as possible. Try out some of the following ideas, which will ensure your Shepherd has an all-round education.

If you are taking on a rescued dog and have little knowledge of his background, it is important to work through a programme of socialisation. A young puppy soaks up new experiences like a sponge, but an older dog can still learn. If a rescued dog shows fear or apprehension, treat him in exactly the same way as you would treat a youngster who is going through the second fear-imprint period (see page 95).

- Accustom your puppy to household noises, such as the vacuum cleaner, the television and the washing machine.
- Ask visitors to come to the door, wearing different types of clothing – for example, wearing a hat or a long raincoat, or carrying a stick or an umbrella.

- If you do not have children at home, make sure your Shepherd has a chance to meet and play with them. Go to a local park and watch children in the play area. You will not be able to take your German Shepherd inside the play area, but he will see children playing and will get used to their shouts of excitement.
- Attend puppy classes. These are designed for puppies between the ages of 12 to 20 weeks, and give puppies a chance to play and interact together in a controlled, supervised environment. Your vet will have details of a local class.
- Take a walk around some quiet streets, such as a residential area, so your Shepherd can get used to the sound of traffic. As he becomes more confident, progress to busier areas.
- Go to a railway station. You don't have to get on a train if you don't need to, but your German Shepherd will have the chance to experience trains, people wheeling luggage, loudspeaker announcements, and going up and down stairs and over railway bridges.
- If you live in the town, plan a trip to the country. You can enjoy a day out and provide an opportunity for your German Shepherd to see livestock, such as sheep, cattle and horses.
- One of the best places for socialising a dog is at a country fair. There will be crowds of people, livestock in pens, tractors, bouncy castles, fairground rides and food stalls.

AN OUTSTANDING TEMPERAMENT

A well-socialised German Shepherd is a tolerant animal
who will take every new situation in his stride.

- When your dog is over 20 weeks of age, find a training class for adult dogs. You may find that your local training class has both puppy and adult classes.

TRAINING CLUBS

There are lots of training clubs to choose from. Your vet will probably have details of clubs in your area, or you can ask friends who have dogs if they attend a club. Alternatively, use the internet to find out more information. But how do you know if the club is any good?

Before you take your dog, ask if you can go to a class as an observer and find out the following:
- What experience does the instructor(s) have?
- Do they have experience with German Shepherds?

- Is the class well organised and are the dogs reasonably quiet? (A noisy class indicates an unruly atmosphere, which will not be conducive to learning.)
- Are there are a number of classes to suit dogs of different ages and abilities?
- Are positive, reward-based training methods used?
- Does the club train for the Good Citizen Scheme (see page 106).

If you are not happy with the training club, find another one. An inexperienced instructor who cannot handle a number of dogs in a confined environment can do more harm than good.

THE ADOLESCENT GERMAN SHEPHERD

It happens to every dog – and every owner. One minute you have an obedient well-behaved youngster, and the next you have a boisterous adolescent who appears to have forgotten everything he learnt. This applies equally to males and females, although the type of adolescent behaviour, and its onset, varies between individuals.

In most cases a German Shepherd male will hit adolescence at around 12-14 months, and you can expect behavioural changes for at least a couple of months. At this time, a male may go through a macho period, believing he is the great 'I am'. He may be bolshie with his owner, and ignore basic commands. The Shepherd is a highly intelligent dog, and you will need to be on your toes as he tests his boundaries. Female Shepherds show adolescent behaviour as they approach their

A training class will teach your dog to behave in the company of other dogs.

first season. The age at which this occurs varies enormously: a bitch may be as young as six months or as old as 14 months before she has her first season. Generally, a female is not as challenging as a male during adolescence, but she may well be moody as hormonal changes influence her behaviour.

When you are coping with an adolescent male, you need to see the world from his perspective. He feels the need to flex his muscles and challenge the status quo. He may become disobedient and break house rules as he tests your authority and your role as leader. Your response must be firm, fair and consistent. If you show that you are a strong leader (see page 84) and are quick to reward good behaviour, your German Shepherd will accept you as his protector and provider.

It is natural for an adolescent dog to test the boundaries.

WHEN THINGS GO WRONG

Positive, reward-based training has proved to be the most effective method of teaching dogs, but what happens when your German Shepherd does something wrong and you need to show him that his behaviour is unacceptable?

The old-fashioned school of dog training used to rely on the powers of punishment and negative reinforcement. A dog who raided the bin, for example, was smacked. Now we have learnt that it is not only unpleasant and cruel to hit a dog, it is also ineffective. If you hit a dog for stealing, he is more than likely to see you as the bad consequence of stealing, so he may raid the bin

again, but probably not when you are around. If he raided the bin some time before you discovered it, he will be even more confused by your punishment, as he will not relate your response to his 'crime'.

A more commonplace example is when a dog fails to respond to a recall in the park. When the dog eventually comes back, the owner puts the dog on the lead and goes straight home to punish the dog for his poor response. Unfortunately, the dog will have a different interpretation. He does not think: "I won't ignore a recall command because the bad consequence is the end of my play in the park." He thinks: "Coming to my owner resulted in the end of playtime – therefore coming to my owner has a bad consequence,

so I won't do that again."

There are a number of strategies to tackle undesirable behaviour – and they have nothing to do with harsh handling.

Ignoring bad behaviour: The German Shepherd has a tendency to be attention seeking, and he can be quite inventive in how he makes his presence felt. A Shepherd may jump up at you, or he may bark continually while you are on the phone or if you are talking to a visitor. The simplest solution is to ignore the behaviour you don't like and reward the behaviour you want. For example, if your Shepherd starts barking to gain your attention, do not look at him and do not speak to him – these actions are rewarding, and the louder you shout, the more rewarding it is. But someone who

If you catch your German Shepherd red-handed, you need to put an instant stop to his behaviour.

turns their back on him and offers no response is plain boring. The moment your German Shepherd is quiet, give him lots of praise and maybe a treat. If you repeat this often enough, the Shepherd will learn that barking does not have any good consequences, such as getting attention. Instead he is ignored. However, when he is quiet, he gets loads of attention. He links the action with the consequence, and chooses the action that is most rewarding. Being ignored is a worst-case scenario for a German Shepherd, so remember to use it as an effective training tool.

Stopping bad behaviour: There are occasions when you want to call an instant halt to whatever it is your German Shepherd is doing. He may have just jumped on the sofa, or you may have caught him red-handed in the rubbish bin. He has already committed the 'crime', so your aim is to stop him and to redirect his attention.

You can do this by using a deep, firm tone of voice to say "No", which will startle him, and then call him to you in a bright, happy voice. If necessary, you can attract him with a toy or a treat. The moment your Shepherd stops the

undesirable behaviour and comes towards you, you can reward his good behaviour. You can back this up by running through a couple of simple exercises, such as a Sit or a Down, and rewarding with treats. In this way, your German Shepherd focuses his attention on you, and sees you as the greatest source of reward and pleasure.

In a more extreme situation, when you want to interrupt undesirable behaviour, and you know that a simple "No" will not do the trick, you can try something a little more dramatic. If you get a can and fill it with pebbles, it will make a really loud noise when you shake it or throw it. The same effect can be achieved with purpose-made training discs. The dog will be startled and stop what he is doing. Even better, the dog will not associate the unpleasant noise with you. This gives you the perfect opportunity to be the nice guy, calling the dog to you and giving him lots of praise.

PROBLEM BEHAVIOUR
If you have trained your German Shepherd from puppyhood, survived his adolescence and established yourself as a firm, fair and consistent leader, you will end up with a brilliant companion dog. The German Shepherd is biddable, eager to please, and loves spending time with his owners. A Shepherd who understands and respects his position in the family hierarchy has no need to show challenging or difficult behaviour.

However, problems may arise

unexpectedly, or you may have taken on a rescued German Shepherd that has established behavioural problems. If you are worried about your Shepherd and feel out of your depth, do not delay in seeking professional help. This is readily available, usually through a referral from your vet, or you can find additional information on the internet (see Appendices for web addresses). An animal behaviourist will have experience in tackling problem behaviour and will be able to help both you and your dog.

MOUTHING

This behaviour is not uncommon in German Shepherds, and unless it is nipped in the bud, it can develop into a severe problem. An adult dog who thinks it is OK to grab hold of your arm is a menace to live with, and if his mouthing gets out of hand, he could inflict serious injury.

A puppy uses his mouth as a means of exploring, and he may nip his mother or littermates when he is playing. The pup's mother will respond with a growl if she is nipped – an instant warning that tells the pup that his behaviour is unacceptable. In the rough and tumble between littermates, a pup who gets nipped will squeal to tell his littermate to let go. When a puppy arrives in his new home, he may treat his human family like his littermates, and mouth or nip as a way of playing. The Shepherd must learn that this behaviour is not acceptable. The best method is to startle the puppy so that he

stops what he is doing instantly. You then have the opportunity to ask for a behaviour you want, such as a "Sit" or a "Down", which you can reward.

It may work if you give a sharp cry to startle your puppy. This is effective with many young puppies of different breeds, but Shepherd puppies are not always responsive to it. If possible, recruit a helper who can stand out of the puppy's sight, armed with training discs or a can filled with pebbles. Play with your puppy, and the instant he starts to mouth, the

helper throws the training discs/can. The puppy will be startled by the noise, which will interrupt his behaviour, but he will not associate the sound with you.

If this habit has not been curbed in puppyhood, it will be harder to break. However, it is important to persevere or you will end up with a potentially dangerous situation.

SEPARATION ANXIETY

The German Shepherd is a loyal and loving dog, and while it may be flattering to think he pines if

A rescued dog may need extra training to overcome behavioural problems.

you are out of sight, it does not result in a happy contented dog. A Shepherd must learn that he can cope on his own, confident in the knowledge that his owner will return.

A puppy should be left for short periods on his own, ideally in a crate where he cannot get up to any mischief. It is a good idea to leave him with a boredom-busting toy (see page 56) so he will be happily occupied in your absence. When you return, do not rush to the crate and make a huge fuss. Wait a few minutes and then calmly go to the crate and release your dog, telling him how good he has been. If this scenario is repeated a number of times, your German Shepherd will soon learn that being left on his own is no big deal.

Problems with separation anxiety are most likely to arise if you take on a rescued dog who has major insecurities. You may also find that your German Shepherd hates being left if you have failed to accustom him to short periods of isolation when he was growing up. Separation anxiety is expressed in a number of ways, and all are equally distressing for both dog and owner. An anxious dog who is left alone may bark and whine continuously, urinate and defecate, and may be extremely destructive.

There are a number of steps you can take when attempting to solve this problem.

- Put up a baby-gate between adjoining rooms, and leave your dog in one room while you are in the other room. Your dog will be able to see you and hear you, but he is learning to cope without being right next to you. Build up the amount of time you can leave your dog in easy stages.
- Buy some boredom-busting toys and fill them with some tasty treats. Whenever you leave your dog, give him a food-filled toy so that he is busy while you are away.

- If you have not used a crate before, it is not too late to start. Make sure the crate is big and comfortable, and train your German Shepherd to get used to going in his crate while you are in the same room. Gradually build up the amount of time he spends in the crate, and then start leaving the room for short periods. When you return, do not make a fuss of your dog. Leave him for five or 10 minutes before releasing him so that he gets used to your comings and goings.
- Pretend to go out, putting on your coat and jangling your keys, but do not leave the house. An anxious dog often becomes hyped-up by the ritual of leave taking, so this will help to desensitize him.
- When you do need to leave the house, do not spend ages reassuring your dog and telling him you'll be back soon. He will not understand what you are saying, but will tune into your anxiety and believe that

A dog that is not used to spending time on his own may become anxious, which could result in destructive behaviour.

something bad is going to happen. Simply put your Shepherd in his crate 10-15 minutes before you are due to go out, allow him to settle, and leave the house calmly and quietly. There is no need for big farewells.

- When you go out, try leaving a radio or a TV on. Some dogs are comforted by hearing voices and background noise when they are left alone.
- Try to make your absences as short as possible when you are first training your dog to accept being on his own. When you return, do not fuss your dog, rushing to his crate to release him. Leave him for a few minutes, and, when you go to him, remain calm and relaxed so that he does not become hyped-up with a huge greeting.

If you take these steps, your dog should become less anxious, and, over a period of time, you should be able to solve the problem. However, if you are failing to make progress, do not delay in calling in expert help.

If your German Shepherd can see you - and you can still talk to him - he will start learning to cope with being on his own.

CLINGY SHEPHERDS
It is sometimes said that the German Shepherd is a 'one person' dog and will not thrive in a family situation, as he focuses all his attention on 'the chosen one'. If you want this type of relationship, a Shepherd will give you his loyalty, but he will be happier if he's an integral member of the family, interacting with everyone who lives in your home. On a purely practical level, a Shepherd who becomes too dependent on one person is likely to become anxious when that person is absent.

There are a number of steps to take to ensure a Shepherd relates to all members of his family:

- Do not let one person, and only one person, feed him. If the job is shared, your Shepherd will respect all family members as providers of his food.
- If you have children, help them to train a few basic exercises, so your Shepherd knows he must obey everyone in the family.
- When your Shepherd needs to be groomed, take it in turns so that your Shepherd allows everyone to handle him.
- Make sure that everyone is consistent with house rules, such as not allowing your Shepherd on the sofa or not letting him jump up, so that he gets a clear message and understands his place in the family.

If you are training your German Shepherd in a canine sport, such as competitive obedience or working trials, he may well look on you as his 'special person' while you are training, but if he is reared correctly, he will remain loving and loyal to all members of his human family.

DOMINANCE
If you have trained and socialised your German Shepherd correctly, he will know his place in the

Incorporate your German Shepherd into family life rather than allowing him to become too dependent on one person.

family pack and will have no desire to challenge your authority. As we have seen, adolescent dogs test the boundaries, and this is the time to enforce all your earlier training so your Shepherd accepts that he is not top dog.

German Shepherds are powerful animals, and males, in particular, may be over-assertive unless they are handled with a reasonable degree of firmness. If you have taken on a rescued dog who has not been trained and socialised, or if you have let your adolescent German Shepherd rule the roost, you may find you have problems with a dominant dog.

Dominance is expressed in many different ways, which may include the following:

• Showing lack of respect for your personal space. For example, your dog will barge through doors ahead of you or jump up at you.

• Getting up on to the sofa or your favourite armchair, and growling when you tell him to get back on the floor.

• Becoming possessive over a toy, or guarding his food bowl by growling when you get too close.

• Growling when anyone approaches his bed or when anyone gets too close to where he is lying.

• Ignoring basic obedience commands, and pulling on the lead.

• Showing no respect to younger members of the family, pushing amongst them, and completely ignoring them.

• Male dogs may start marking (cocking their leg) in the house.

• Aggression towards people (see page 105).

If you see signs of your German Shepherd becoming too dominant, you must work at lowering his status so that he realises that you are the leader and he must accept your authority. Although you need to be firm, you also need to use positive training methods so that your Shepherd is rewarded for the behaviour you want. In this way, his 'correct' behaviour will be strengthened and repeated.

There are a number of steps you can take to lower your German Shepherd's status. They include:

• Go back to basics and hold daily training sessions. Make sure you have some really tasty treats, or find a toy your German Shepherd really values and only bring it out at training sessions. Run through all the training exercises you have taught your Shepherd. Make a big fuss of him and reward him when he does well. This will reinforce the message that you are the leader and that it is rewarding to do as you ask.

- Teach your German Shepherd something new; this can be as simple as learning a trick, such as shaking paws. Having something new to think about will mentally stimulate your Shepherd, and he will benefit from interacting with you.

- Be 100 per cent consistent with all house rules – your German Shepherd must never sit on the sofa, and you must never allow him to bark as a way of getting your attention.

- If your German Shepherd has been guarding his food bowl, put the bowl down empty and drop in a little food at a time. Allow your Shepherd to eat when you give a command, such as "OK". When he has finished, give it a few seconds, and then reward him by dropping in more food. This shows your German Shepherd that you are the provider of the food, and he can only eat when you allow him to.

- Make sure the family eats before you feed your Shepherd. Some trainers advocate eating in front of the dog (maybe just a few bites from a biscuit) before starting a training session, so the dog appreciates your elevated status.

- Do not let your German Shepherd barge through doors ahead of you or leap from the back of the car before you release him. You may need to put your dog on the lead and teach him to "Wait" at doorways, and then reward him

There are times when a Shepherd may seek to challenge your authority, and will deliberately break house rules.

for letting you go through first.

- Be aloof towards your dog. He will learn that he has to do something for a reward – even affection is not given freely.

If your German Shepherd is progressing well with his retraining programme, think about getting involved with a dog sport, such as agility, competitive obedience or working trials. This will give your Shepherd a positive outlet for his energies. However, if your German Shepherd is still seeking to be dominant, or you have any other concerns, do not delay in seeking the help of an animal behaviourist.

AGGRESSION

Aggression is a complex issue, as there are different causes and the behaviour may be triggered by numerous factors. It may be

directed towards people, but far more commonly it is directed towards other dogs. Aggression in dogs may be the result of:

- **Dominance** (see page 103).
- **Defensive behaviour:** This may be induced by fear, pain or punishment.
- **Territory:** A dog may become aggressive if strange dogs or people enter his territory (which is generally seen as the house and garden).
- **Intra-sexual issues:** This is aggression between sexes – male-to-male or female-to-female.
- **Parental instinct:** A mother dog may become aggressive if she is protecting her puppies.

A dog who has been well socialised (see page 94) and has been given sufficient exposure to other dogs at significant stages of

If you are experiencing problems with your German Shepherd, divert his energies – and intelligence – into learning something new, so you can reward good behaviour.

his development will rarely be aggressive. A well-bred German Shepherd that has been reared correctly should not have a hint of aggression in his temperament. Obviously if you have taken on an older, rescued dog, you will have little or no knowledge of his background, and if he shows signs of aggression, the cause will need to be determined. In most cases, you would be well advised to call in professional help if you see aggressive behaviour in your dog; if the aggression is directed towards people, you should seek immediate advice. This behaviour can escalate very quickly and could lead to disastrous consequences.

NEW CHALLENGES

If you enjoy training your German Shepherd, you may want to try one of the many dog sports that are now on offer.

GOOD CITIZEN SCHEME

This is a scheme run by the Kennel Club in the UK and the American Kennel Club in the USA. The schemes promote responsible ownership and help you to train a well-behaved dog who will fit in with the community. The schemes are excellent for all pet owners, and they are also a good starting point if you plan to compete with your German Shepherd when he is older. The KC and the AKC

schemes vary in format. In the UK there are three levels – bronze, silver and gold – with each test becoming progressively more demanding. In the AKC scheme there is a single test.

Some of the exercises include:
- Walking on a loose lead among people and other dogs.
- Recall amid distractions.
- A controlled greeting where dogs stay under control while owners meet.
- The dog allows all-over grooming and handling by the owner and also accepts being handled by the examiner.
- Stays, with the owner in sight, and then out of sight.
- Food manners, allowing the owner to eat without begging, and taking a treat on command.
- Sendaway – sending the dog to his bed.

The tests are designed to show the control you have over your dog, and his ability to respond correctly and remain calm in all situations. The Good Citizen Scheme is taught at most training clubs. For more information, log on to the Kennel Club or AKC website (see Appendices).

SHOWING

In your eyes, your German Shepherd is the most beautiful dog in the world – but would a judge agree? Showing is a highly competitive sport and as the German Shepherd is a popular breed, classes tend to be big. However, many owners get bitten by the showing bug, and their calendar is governed by the dates of the top showing fixtures.

To be successful in the show ring, a German Shepherd must conform as closely as possible to the Breed Standard, which is a written blueprint describing the 'perfect' German Shepherd (see Chapter Seven). To get started you need to buy a puppy that has show potential and then train him to perform in the ring. A German Shepherd will be expected to stand in show pose, gait for the judge in order to show off his natural movement, and to be examined by the judge. This involves a detailed hands-on examination, so your Shepherd must be bombproof when handled by strangers.

Many training clubs hold ringcraft classes, which are run by experienced showgoers. At these classes, you will learn how to handle your German Shepherd in the ring, and you will also find out about rules, procedures and show ring etiquette.

The best plan is to start off at some small, informal shows where you can practise and learn the tricks of the trade before graduating to bigger shows. It's a long haul starting in the very first puppy class, but the dream is to make your German Shepherd up into a Champion.

COMPETITIVE OBEDIENCE

Border Collies dominate this sport, but German Shepherds are also well represented and can produce work of the highest standard. A Shepherd will focus intently on his handler, and, in time, will develop the

Showing is highly competitive at the top level, but it can be rewarding if you have a German Shepherd of quality.

concentration and accuracy that is required. The classes start off being relatively easy and become progressively more challenging with additional exercises and the handler giving minimal instructions to the dog.

Exercises include:

- **Heelwork:** Dog and handler must complete a set pattern on and off the lead, which includes left turns, right turns, about turns, and changes of pace.
- **Recall:** This may be when the handler is stationary or on the move.
- **Retrieve:** This may be a dumbbell or any article chosen by the judge.
- **Sendaway:** The dog is sent to a designated spot and must go into an instant Down until he is recalled by the handler.
- **Stays:** The dog must stay in the Sit and in the Down for a set amount of time. In advanced classes, the handler is out of sight.

- **Scent:** The dog must retrieve a single cloth from a pre-arranged pattern of cloths that has his owner's scent, or, in advanced classes, the judge's scent. There may also be decoy cloths.
- **Distance control.** The dog must execute a series of moves (Sit, Stand, Down) without moving from his position and with the handler at a distance.

Even though competitive obedience requires accuracy and precision, it should also be fun for your German Shepherd, so give lots of praise and rewards to motivate him to do his best. Many training clubs run advanced classes for those who want to compete in obedience or you can hire the services of a professional trainer for one-on-one sessions.

AGILITY

This fun sport has grown enormously in popularity over the past few years. If you fancy having

The German Shepherd is one of the most successful breeds in competitive obedience.

Protection is the third element of Schutzhund.

a go, make sure you have good control over your German Shepherd and keep him slim. Agility is a very physical sport, which demands fitness from both dog and handler. A fat Shepherd is never going to make it as an agility competitor.

In agility competitions, each dog must complete a set course over a series of obstacles, which include:

- Jumps (upright hurdles and long jump)
- Weaves
- A-frame
- Dog walk
- Seesaw
- Tunnels (collapsible and rigid)
- Tyre

Dogs may compete in Jumping classes with jumps, tunnels and weaves, or in Agility Classes, which have the full set of equipment. Faults are awarded for poles down on the jumps, missed contact points on the A-frame, dog walk and seesaw, and refusals. If a dog takes the wrong course, he is eliminated. The winner is the dog that completes the course in the fastest time with no faults. As you progress up the grades, courses become progressively harder with more twists, turns and changes of direction.

If you want to get involved in agility, you will need to find a club that specialises in the sport (see Appendices). You will not be allowed to start training until your German Shepherd is 12 months old, and you cannot compete until he is 18 months old. This rule is for the protection of the dog, who may suffer injury if he puts strain on bones and joints while he is still growing.

WORKING TRIALS

This is a very challenging sport, and it is tailormade for the versatile and talented German Shepherd Dog. The sport consists of three basic components:

- **Control:** Dog and handler must complete obedience exercises, but the work does not have to be as precise as it is in competitive obedience. In the advanced classes, manwork (where the dog works as a guard/protection dog) is a major feature.
- **Agility:** The dog must negotiate a 3 ft (0.91 m) hurdle, a 9 ft (2.75 m) long jump, and a 6 ft (1.82) upright scale, which is the most taxing piece of dog equipment.
- **Nosework:** The dog must follow a track that has been laid over a set course. The surface

A well-trained, well-socialised German Shepherd is a joy to own.

may vary, and the length of time between the track being laid and the dog starting work is increased in the advanced classes.

The ladder of stakes are: Companion Dog, Utility Dog, Working Dog, Tracking Dog and Patrol Dog. In the US, tracking is a sport in its own right, and is very popular among German Shepherd owners.

If you want to get involved in working trials, you will need to find a specialist club or a trainer specialiing in this field. For more information, see Appendices.

SCHUTZHUND
Schutzhund is another popular sport in which many German Shepherds participate, particularly in the breed's native Germany. The name comes from the German word meaning 'protection dog'.

Schutzhund originated in Germany to test the temperament and ability of the German Shepherd Dog, ensuring that only quality dogs were bred from. Today it is practised worldwide.

There are three disciplines involved in Schutzhund – tracking, obedience and

protection. In effect, Schutzhund is a 'triathlon' for working dogs.

SUMMING UP
The German Shepherd Dog is one of the most popular companion dogs in the world, and deservedly so. He has an outstanding temperament: he is loyal, highly intelligent, and fun to live with. Make sure you keep your half of the bargain: spend time socialising and training your Shepherd so that you can be proud to take him anywhere, and he will always be a credit to you.

THE PERFECT GERMAN SHEPHERD DOG

Chapter 7

The Breed Standard is the 'blueprint' of the ideal specimen in each breed, which is approved by a governing body, such as the Kennel Club, the Fédération Cynologique Internationale (FCI) and the American Kennel Club.

THE KENNEL CLUB

The Kennel Club writes and revises Breed Standards, taking account of the advice of breed councils/clubs. Breed Standards are not changed lightly, to avoid 'changing the Standard to fit the current dogs' and the health and well-being of future dogs is always taken into account when new Standards are prepared or existing ones altered. The Kennel Club Standards are concise, uniform in structure and provide a basic description of the perfect specimen.

The Standard was last changed in October 2009 to incorporate the KC's 'fit for purpose' clause, which states: "*Breeders and judges should at all times be careful to avoid obvious conditions or exaggerations which would be detrimental in any way to the health, welfare or soundness of this breed.*" It goes on to add: "*If a feature or quality is desirable it should only be present in the right measure.*"

THE FÉDÉRATION CYNOLOGIQUE INTERNATIONALE (FCI)

The aims of the FCI are to encourage and promote the breeding and use of purebred dogs whose functional health and physical features meet the Standard set for each respective breed and who are capable of working and accomplishing functions in accordance with the specific characteristics of their breed. The FCI also aims to protect the use, keeping and breeding of dogs in the member countries; to support free exchange of dogs and cynological information between member countries; and to initiate the organisation of exhibitions and tests.

THE AMERICAN KENNEL CLUB

The American Kennel Club is dedicated to upholding the integrity of its registry, promoting the sport of purebred dogs and breeding type and function.

Although these three main organisations have the same aims regarding the breed, their printed Standards vary. Therefore, can a Standard contain every detail of the dog? Can it give a complete picture of what the German Shepherd Dog should look like?

Most newcomers cannot accurately interpret the Breed Standard and therefore receive insufficient guidance from it. Most Breed Standards assume you have a working knowledge of the breed, and also a familiarity with the terms most commonly used in dog breeding. Like most professions and hobbies, there is a language that must be learned before you can attempt to understand and learn.

However, beauty is in the eye of the beholder and we can all interpret words to the way our minds and eyes tell us. Over the years the breed has been influenced by German-, English- and American-type dogs, yet the Breed Standard does not advocate dramatic difference in type.

Study the following four pictures. Which, in your opinion, interprets a correct German Shepherd Dog according to the Breed Standard, as you know it? All four dogs are from different decades; all must have conformed to the Standard according to the judges who awarded these dogs the title of Champion. Do they differ that much according to the interpretation of the Standard? Underneath the coat, skin and muscle, the German Shepherd Dog skeleton does not differ.

In order to better understand what makes a 'perfect' German Shepherd Dog, the British (KC), American (AKC) and Fédération Cynologique Internationale (FCI) Breed Standards are reproduced and analysed with special pictorial reference.

The 'perfect' German Shepherd Dog – as judged in different decades, compared to the unchanging, underlying skeleton.

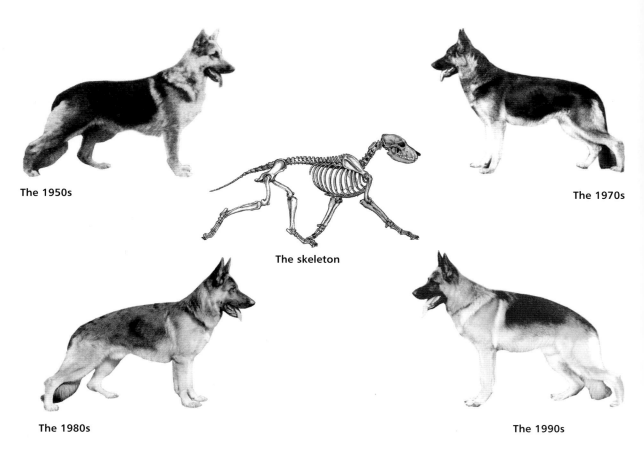

The 1950s

The 1970s

The skeleton

The 1980s

The 1990s

THE INTERNATIONAL GERMAN SHEPHERD DOG

The English, American and FCI Breed Standards vary slightly in detail,
but all breeders should be aiming for the same blueprint.

A top-winning Champion in the UK.

A highly successful dog in the American show ring.

A top-quality German Shepherd Dog now being shown in Germany.

GENERAL APPEARANCE

KC

Slightly long in comparison to height; of powerful, well muscled build with weather-resistant coat. Relation between height, length, position and structure of fore and hindquarters (angulation) producing far-reaching, enduring gait. Clear definition of masculinity and femininity essential, and working ability never sacrificed for mere beauty.

AKC

The first impression of a good German Shepherd Dog is that of a strong, agile, well muscled animal, alert and full of life. It is well balanced, with harmonious development of the forequarter and hindquarter. The dog is longer than tall, deep-bodied, and presents an outline of smooth curves rather than angles. It looks substantial and not spindly, giving the impression, both at rest and in motion, of muscular fitness and nimbleness without any look of clumsiness or soft living. The ideal dog is stamped with a look of quality and nobility – difficult to define, but unmistakable when present. Secondary sex characteristics are strongly marked, and every animal gives a definite impression of masculinity or femininity, according to its sex.

FCI

The German Shepherd is slightly long, strong and well muscled. The bones are dry and the structure firm. The ratio of height to length and the placement and structure of the limbs (angulation) are so balanced that a far-reaching, effortless trot is guaranteed. He has a weather proof coat.

A pleasing appearance is desired as long as the working ability of the dog is not called into question.

Sex characteristics must be pronounced, e.g., the masculinity of the males and the femininity of the females must be unmistakable.

The German Shepherd that corresponds to the Standard offers the observer a picture of rugged strength, intelligence and agility, whose overall proportions are neither in excess nor deficient in any way. The way he moves and behaves leaves no doubt that he is sound in mind and body and so possesses physical and mental traits that render possible an every-ready working dog with great stamina.

It is only possible for a practised expert to ascertain the presence of requisite working dog traits in the German Shepherd. Therefore, only special judges should be called upon, as it is incumbent on them to judge the character of the dogs brought before them. This should include a test for gun soundness, as only German Shepherd Dogs that have achieved recognised working dog titles may receive the breed rating excellent.

With an effervescent temperament, the dog must also be cooperative, adapting to every situation, and take to work willingly and joyfully. He must show courage and hardness as the situation requires to defend his handler and his property. He must readily attack on his owner's command but otherwise be a fully attentive, obedient and pleasant household companion. He should be devoted to his familiar surroundings, above all to other animals and children, and composed in his contact with people. All in all, he gives a harmonious picture of natural nobility and self-confidence.

The immediate impression of the GSD is of a dog slightly long in comparison to its height, with a powerful and well-muscled body. The coat should be weatherproof.

He should give an innate impression of strength, intelligence and suppleness. His manner should demonstrate that he is perfectly sound in mind and body, and has the physical and mental attributes to make him always ready for action as a working dog.

He must be tractable enough to adapt in different situations, showing vitality, enthusiasm and willingness to work. He must be courageous and possess the determination to defend himself and his master if ever required. With the attributes of nobility, alertness and self-confidence he will be an observant, obedient member of the household, especially with children.

CHARACTERISTICS AND TEMPERAMENT

KC
Versatile working dog, balanced and free from exaggeration. Attentive, alert, resilient and tireless with keen scenting ability.

Steady of nerve, loyal, self-assured, courageous and tractable. Never nervous, over-aggressive or shy.

AKC
The breed has a distinct personality marked by direct and fearless, but not hostile, expression, self-confidence and a certain aloofness that does not lend itself to immediate and indiscriminate friendships. The dog must be approachable, quietly standing its ground and showing confidence and willingness to meet overtures without itself making them. It is poised, but when the occasion demands, eager and alert; both fit and willing to serve in its capacity as companion, watchdog, blind leader, herding dog, or guardian, whichever the circumstances may demand.

The dog must not be timid, shrinking behind its master or handler; it should not be nervous, looking about or upward with anxious

The courageous, yet steady, temperament has made the German Shepherd the chosen breed for police and security work.

expression or showing nervous reactions, such as tucking of tail, to strange sounds or sights. Lack of confidence under any surroundings is not typical of good character.

Any of the above deficiencies in character which indicate shyness must be penalized as very serious faults and any dog exhibiting pronounced indications of these must be excused from the ring. It must be possible for the judge to observe the teeth and to determine that both testicles are descended.

Any dog that attempts to bite the judge must be disqualified. The ideal dog is a working animal with an incorruptible character combined with body

and gait suitable for the arduous work that constitutes its primary purpose.

FCI
Sound nerves, alertness, self-confidence, trainability, watchfulness, loyalty and incorruptibility, as well as courage, fighting drive and hardness, are the outstanding characteristics of a purebred German Shepherd Dog. They make him suitable to be a superior working dog in general, and in particular to be a guard, companion, protection and herding dog.

His ample scenting abilities, added to his conformation as a trotter, make it possible for him to quietly and surely work out a track without bodily strain and with his nose close to the ground. This makes him highly useful as a multi-purpose track and search dog.

The main characteristics of the GSD are: steadiness of nerves, attentiveness, loyalty, calm self-assurance, alertness and tractability, as well as courage with physical resilience and scenting ability. These characteristics are necessary for a versatile working dog. Nervousness, over-aggressiveness, and shyness are very serious faults.

SIZE, PROPORTION AND SUBSTANCE

KC

Ideal height (from withers and just touching elbows): dogs: 63 cms (25 ins); bitches: 58 cms (23 ins). 2.5 cms (1 in) either above or below ideal permissible.

AKC

The desired height for males at the top of the highest point of the shoulder blade is 24 to 26 inches; and for bitches, 22 to 24 inches.

The German Shepherd Dog is longer than tall, with the most desirable proportion as 10 to 8½.

The length is measured from the point of the prosternum or breastbone to the rear edge of the pelvis, the ischial tuberosity.

The desirable long proportion is not derived from a long back, but from overall length with relation to height, which is achieved by length of forequarter and length of withers and hindquarter, viewed from the side.

FCI

The German Shepherd Dog is medium sized. With the hair pressed down, the height at the withers is measured by stick along the vertical as it follows the line of the elbow from the withers to the ground. The ideal height at the withers is 62.5 cm for males and 57.5 for females. An allowance of 2.5 cm over or under is permissible. Exceeding the maximum as well as not meeting the minimum diminishes the working and breeding value of the dog.

The German Shepherd Dog is a medium-sized breed. We are looking for slightly stretched proportions of, ideally, a ratio of 10-9 or 10-8.5, with a depth of brisket 45-48 per cent. Withers height is determined at the upper tips of the shoulder blade.

In order to adhere to the Breed Standard and fulfil his role as a working dog, he should be both mentally and physically strong.

HEAD AND SKULL

KC

Proportionate in size to body, never coarse, too fine or long. Clean cut; fairly broad between ears. Forehead slightly domed; little or no trace of central furrow. Cheeks forming softly rounded curve, never protruding. Skull from ears to bridge of nose tapering gradually and evenly, blending without too pronounced stop into wedge-shaped powerful muzzle. Skull approximately 50 per cent of overall length of head. Width of skull corresponding approximately to length, in males slightly

Correct ear carriage: Set high and erect.

greater, in females slightly less. Muzzle strong, lips firm, clean and closing tightly. Top of muzzle straight, almost parallel to forehead. Short, blunt, weak, pointed, overlong muzzle undesirable.
Eyes: Medium-sized, almond-shaped, never protruding. Dark brown preferred, lighter shade permissible, provided expression good and general harmony of head not destroyed. Expression lively, intelligent and self-assured.
Ears: Medium-sized, firm in texture, broad at base, set high, carried erect, almost parallel, never pulled inwards or tipped, tapering to a point, open at front. Never hanging. Folding back during movement permissible.
Mouth: Jaws strongly developed. With a perfect, regular and complete scissor bite, i.e. upper teeth closely overlapping lower teeth and set square to the jaws. Teeth healthy and strong. Full dentition desirable.

AKC

The head is noble, cleanly chiseled, strong without coarseness, but above all not fine, and in proportion to the body. The head of the male is distinctly masculine, and that of the bitch distinctly feminine.
Eyes: The expression keen, intelligent and composed. Eyes of medium size, almond shaped, set a little obliquely

Incorrect ear carriage: Set slightly high (left) and slightly wide (right).

and not protruding. The color is as dark as possible.
Ears: The ears are moderately pointed, in proportion to the skull, open toward the front, and carried erect when at attention, the ideal carriage being one in which the center lines of the ears, viewed from the front, are parallel to each other and perpendicular to the ground. A dog with cropped or hanging ears must be disqualified.
Muzzle: Seen from the front the forehead is only moderately arched, and the skull slopes into the long, wedge-shaped muzzle without abrupt stop. The muzzle is long and strong, and its topline is parallel to the topline of the skull.
Nose: The nose is black. A dog with a nose that is not predominantly black must be disqualified.
Mouth: The lips are firmly fitted. Jaws are strongly developed. Teeth – 42 in number – 20 upper and 22 lower – are strongly developed and meet in a scissors bite in

which part of the inner surface of the upper incisors meet and engage part of the outer surface of the lower incisors. An overshot jaw or a level bite is undesirable. An undershot jaw is a disqualifying fault. Complete dentition is to be preferred. Any missing teeth other than first premolars is a serious fault.

FCI

The head should be in proportion to the body size (in length approximately 40% of the height at the withers) and not coarse, over refined or overstretched (snipey). In general appearance, it should be dry with moderate breadth between the ears.

The forehead when viewed from the front or side is only slightly arched. It should be without a centre furrow or with only a slightly defined furrow.

The cheeks form a gentle curve laterally without protrusion toward the front. When viewed from above, the skull (approximately 50% of the entire head length) tapers

The male head (left) should look distinctly masculine compared to the softer, more feminine, female head.

gradually and evenly from the ears to the tip of the nose, with a sloping rather than a sharply defined stop and into a long, dry wedge-shaped muzzle (the upper and lower jaws must be strongly developed).

The width of the skull should correspond approximately to the length of the skull. Also, a slight oversize in the case of males or undersize in the case of females is not objectionable.

Eyes: The eyes are of medium size, almond shaped, somewhat slanting and not protruding. The colour of the eyes should blend with the colour of the coat. They should be as dark as possible.

They should have a lively, intelligent and self-confident expression.

Ears: The ears are of medium size, wide at the base and set high. They taper to a point and are carried facing forward and vertically (the tips not inclined toward each other). Tipped, cropped and hanging ears are rejected. Ears drawn toward each other greatly impair the general appearance. The ears of puppies and young dogs sometimes drop or pull toward each other during the teething period, which can last until six months of age and sometimes longer.

Many dogs draw their ears back during motion or at rest. This is not faulty.

Muzzle: The muzzle is strong; the lips are firm and dry and close tightly.

Nose: The bridge of the nose is straight and runs nearly parallel with the plane of the forehead.

Mouth: Dentition must be healthy, strong and complete (42 teeth, 20 in the upper jaw and 22 in the lower jaw). The German Shepherd Dog has a scissors bite, e.g. the incisors must meet each other in a scissors-like fashion, with the outer surface of the incisors of the lower jaw sliding next to the inner surface of the incisors of the upper jaw.

An undershot or overshot bite is faulty, as are large gaps between the teeth. A level bite is faulty, as the incisors close on a straight line.

The jaws must be strongly developed so that the teeth may be deeply rooted.

The head should be in proportion to the body, being of masculine or feminine strength as defined by sex. Muzzle should be 50 per cent of the length of the head with lips dry and well set in. The width at the top of the head should correspond equally to the length of the skull.

Ears are medium size, broad at the base, set high and carried erect, almost parallel, tapering to a point and open at the front. Dark brown eyes are preferred but eyes of a lighter shade are acceptable provided the expression and general harmony of the head is not destroyed.

Two sets of teeth are necessary to accommodate growth and use of teeth for food digestion. The first set are fully erupted and functional early in the second month after birth. These primary teeth, known as deciduous teeth, serve the animal during its puppyhood.

All adult teeth have a function: the canines for grabbing and holding, incisors for nibbling, premolars for tearing, and molars for crushing. However, although they are not used as first intended, they are still necessary for eating modern diets and should be kept healthy and clean.

Playing with toys, bones and feeding the correct type of food can achieve this.

NECK

KC
Fairly long, strong, with well developed muscles, free from throatiness. Carried at 45 degrees angle to horizontal, raised when excited, lowered at fast trot.

AKC
The neck is strong and muscular, clean-cut and relatively long, proportionate in size to the head and without loose folds of skin. When the dog is at attention or excited, the head is raised and the neck carried high; otherwise typical carriage of the head is forward rather than up and but little higher than the top of the shoulders, particularly in motion.

FCI
The neck should be strong with well-developed muscles and without looseness of the throat skin (dewlaps). The neck is carried at an angle of about 45 degrees to the horizontal. It is carried higher when excited and lowered when trotting.

The neck is of good length as it is built upon seven vertebrae. It is strong with well-developed muscles and without looseness of flesh around the throat. The angle of the neck to the body (horizontal) is about 45 degrees

ADULT DENTITION

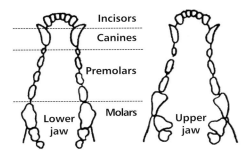

Incisors
Canines
Premolars
Molars
Lower jaw
Upper jaw

BITES

Correct: Scissor bite

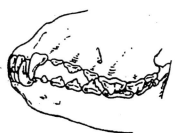

Faulty: Level bite

Faulty: Overshot bite

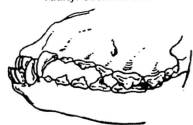

Faulty: Undershot bite

when standing. It is more erect when the dog is excited, and is lower when the dog is trotting.

The withers are located just behind the base of the neck at the neck/back junction. The withers should be defined by a well-laid-back shoulder blade, sloping down smoothly into the back.

FOREQUARTERS

KC

Shoulder blade and upper arms are equal in length, well muscled and firmly attached to the body. Shoulder blades set obliquely (approximately 45 degrees) laid flat to body. Upper arm strong, well muscled, joining shoulder blade at approximately 90 degrees. Seen from all sides,

the forearms are straight and, seen from the front, absolutely parallel. Bone oval rather than round. The elbows must turn neither in nor out while standing or moving. Pasterns firm, supple, with a slight forward slope. An over long, weak pastern, which would affect a dog's working ability is to be heavily penalised. Length of foreleg slightly exceeds the depth of chest.

AKC

The shoulder blades are long and obliquely angled, laid on flat and not placed forward. The upper arm joins the shoulder blade at about a right angle. Both the upper arm and the shoulder blade are well muscled. The forelegs, viewed

from all sides, are straight and the bone oval rather than round. The pasterns are strong and springy and angulated at approximately a 25-degree angle from the vertical. Dewclaws on the forelegs may be removed, but are normally left on.

FCI

The shoulder blade should be long with an oblique placement (the angle at 45 degrees) and lying flat against the body. The upper arm joins the shoulder blade in an approximate right angle. The upper arm as well as the shoulder must be strong and well muscled.

The forearm must be straight when viewed from all sides. The bones of the upper arm and forearm are more oval

CORRECT CONSTRUCTION OF FOREQUARTERS

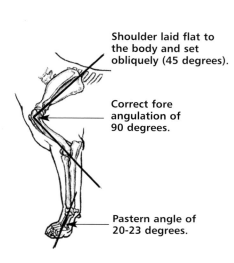

Shoulder laid flat to the body and set obliquely (45 degrees).

Correct fore angulation of 90 degrees.

Pastern angle of 20-23 degrees.

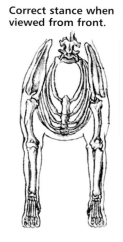

Correct stance when viewed from front.

than round. The pasterns should be firm but neither too steep nor too down in pastern (approximately 20 degrees).

The elbows must be neither turned in nor turned out. The length of the leg bones should exceed the depth of the chest (approximately 55 per cent).

The forequarters consist of a shoulder blade that should be long, set obliquely (at approximately 45 degrees) and laid flat to the body. The upperarm should be strong and well muscled and joined to the shoulder blade (of near equal length) at a near right angle.

The foreleg, from the pasterns to the elbow, should be oval in bone rather than round. The pasterns should be firm and supple and angulated at approximately 20-23 degrees.

When the dog is standing naturally, the elbows are in relatively close proximity to the adjoining chest wall, i.e. well held in, but not so tightly as to restrict movement. An animal in which one or both elbows drift some distance away from the chest wall is referred to as being 'out in elbow or elbows' or 'loose in elbow or elbows'. This often leads to the animal being unsound, exhibiting an energy-wasting and excessively tiring gait. The opposite to this is when the elbows are placed too firmly against the chest wall. This is often associated with a front that is tied in or too narrow between the forelegs.

THE CORRECT PROPORTIONS OF A GERMAN SHEPHERD DOG

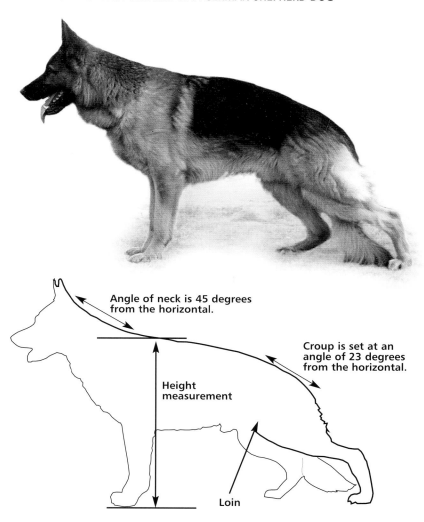

Angle of neck is 45 degrees from the horizontal.

Croup is set at an angle of 23 degrees from the horizontal.

Height measurement

Loin

TOPLINE/ BODY

KC

Length measured from point of shoulder to point of buttock, slightly exceeding height at withers. Correct ratio 10 to 9 or 8 and a half. Undersized dogs, stunted growth, high-legged dogs, those too heavy or too light in build, over-loaded fronts, too short overall appearance, any feature detracting from reach or endurance of gait, undesirable. Chest deep (45-48 per cent) of height at shoulder, not too broad, brisket long, well developed. Ribs well formed and long; neither barrel-shaped nor too flat; allowing free movement of elbows when gaiting. Relatively short loin. Belly firm, only slightly drawn up. Back between withers and croup, straight, strongly developed, not too long. Overall length achieved by correct angle of well laid shoulders, correct length of croup and hindquarters. The topline runs without any visible break from the set on of the neck, over the well defined withers, falling away slightly in a straight line to the gently sloping croup. The back is firm, strong and well muscled. Loin broad, strong, well muscled. Weak, soft and roach backs undesirable and should be heavily penalised. Croup slightly sloping and without any break in the topline, merges imperceptibly with the set on of the tail. Short, steep or flat croups highly undesirable.

AKC

Commencing at the prosternum, the chest is well filled and carried well down between the legs. It is deep and capacious, never shallow, with ample room for lungs and heart, carried well forward, with the prosternum showing ahead of the shoulder in profile.

The withers are higher than and sloping into the level back. The back is straight, very strongly developed without sag or roach, and relatively short. The whole structure of the body gives an impression of depth and solidity without bulkiness.

Ribs well sprung and long, neither barrel-shaped nor too flat, and carried down to a sternum which reaches to the elbows. Correct ribbing allows the elbows to move back freely when the dog is at a trot. Too round causes interference and throws the elbows out; too flat or short causes pinched elbows. Ribbing is carried well back so that the loin is relatively short. Abdomen firmly held and not paunchy. The bottom line is only moderately tucked up in the loin.

Loin: Viewed from the top, broad and strong. Undue length between the last rib and the thigh, when viewed from the side, is undesirable. Croup long and gradually sloping.

FCI

The body length should exceed the height at the withers. It should amount to about 110 to 117% of the height at the withers. Dogs with a short, square or tall build are undesirable.

The chest is deep (approximately 45 to 48 per cent of the height at the withers) but not too wide. The under chest should be as long as possible and pronounced.

The ribs should be well formed and long, neither barrel shaped nor too flat. They should reach the sternum, which is at the same level as the elbows. A correctly formed rib cage allows the elbows freedom of movement when the dog trots. A too round rib cage disrupts the motion of the elbows and causes them to turn out. A too flat rib cage draws the elbows in toward one another. The rib cage extends far back so that the loins are relatively short.

The abdomen is moderately tucked up. The back, including the loins, is straight and strongly developed yet not too long between the withers and the croup.

The withers must be long and high, sloping slightly from front to rear, defined against the back into which it gently blends without breaking the topline.

The loins must be wide, strong and well muscled.

The croup is long and slightly angled (approximately 23 degrees). The ileum and the sacrum are the foundation bones of the croup. Short, steep or flat croups are undesirable.

The back line is the area between the withers and croup; it should be straight, strongly developed and not too long.

The loin is the lumbar area, extending from the end of the ribcage to the start of the pelvis. It should be broad, strong and well muscled, and it should not be too long.

The croup is set at an angle of 23 degrees from the horizontal. It should be of good length, gently curving to the set of the tail.

HINDQUARTERS

KC

Overall strong, broad and well muscled, enabling effortless forward propulsion. Upper and lower thigh are approximately of equal length. Hind angulation sufficient if imaginary line dropped from point of buttocks cuts through lower thigh just in front of hock, continuing down slightly in front of hindfeet. Angulations corresponding approximately with front angulation, without over-angulation. See from rear, the hind legs are straight and parallel to each other. The hocks are strong and firm. The rear pasterns are vertical. Any tendency towards over-angulation of hindquarters, weak hocks, cow hocks or sickle hooks, is to be heavily penalised as this reduces firmness and endurance in movement.

AKC

The whole assembly of the thigh, viewed from the side, is broad, with both upper and lower thigh well muscled, forming as nearly as possible a right angle. The upper thigh bone parallels the shoulder blade while the lower thigh bone parallels the upper arm. The metatarsus (the unit between the hock joint and the foot) is short, strong and tightly articulated. The dewclaws, if any, should be removed from the hind legs.

FCI

The thigh is broad and well muscled. The upper thigh bone when viewed from the side joins the only slightly longer lower thigh bone at an angle of approximately 120 degrees. The angulation corresponds roughly to the forequarter angulation without being overangulated.

The hock is strong and forms a firm joint with the lower thigh. The entire hindquarters must be strong and well muscled to be capable of carrying the body effortlessly forward during motion.

The thighs should be broad and well muscled. The upper thigh bone, viewed from the side, should slope to the lower thigh bone. The angulation should correspond approximately with the front angulation without being over angulated. The hindquarters overall must be strong and well muscled to enable the effortless forward propulsion of the whole body. Any tendency towards over angulation of the hindquarters reduces firmness and endurance.

CORRECT CONSTRUCTION OF HINDQUARTERS

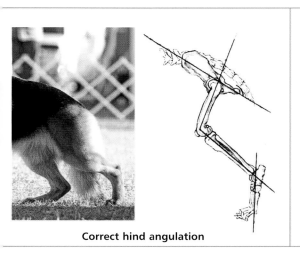

Correct hind angulation

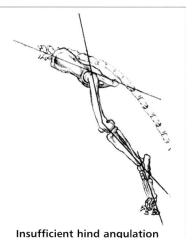

Insufficient hind angulation

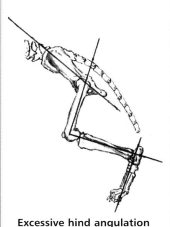

Excessive hind angulation

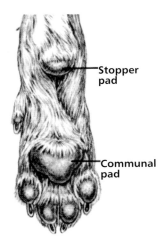

Construction of the foot.

FEET

KC
Rounded toes well closed and arched. Pads well cushioned and durable. Nails short, strong and dark in colour.

AKC
The feet are short, compact with toes well arched, pads thick and firm, nails short and dark.

FCI
The feet are relatively round, short, tightly formed and arched. The pads are very hard, but not chapped. The nails are short, strong and of a dark colour.

Dewclaws sometimes appear on the hind legs and should be removed within the first few days of birth.

The feet have rounded toes that are well closed and arched. The pads are well cushioned and durable. The nails are short, strong and dark in colour.

TAIL

KC
Bushy-haired, reaches at least to hock – ideal length reaching to middle of metatarsus. At rest tail hangs in slight sabre-like curve; when moving raised and curve increased, ideally never above level of back. Short, rolled, curled, generally carried badly or stumpy from birth, undesirable.

AKC
Tail bushy, with the last vertebra extended at least to the hock joint. It is set smoothly into the croup and low rather than high. At rest, the tail hangs in a slight curve like a saber. A slight hook – sometimes carried to one side – is faulty only to the extent that it mars general appearance. When the dog is excited or in motion, the curve is accentuated and the tail raised, but it should never be curled forward beyond a vertical line. Tails too short, or with clumpy ends due to ankylosis, are serious faults. A dog with a docked tail must be disqualified.

FCI
The tail is bushy and should reach at least to the hock joint but not beyond the middle of the hocks. Sometimes the tail forms a hook to one side at its end, though this is undesirable. At rest the tail is carried in a gentle downward curve, but when the dog is excited or in motion, it is curved more and carried higher. The tail should never be raised past the vertical. The tail, therefore, should not be carried straight or curled over the back. Docked tails are inadmissible.

The tail should reach at least as far as the hock joint with a bone structure of 18-23 vertebrae and

TAIL CARRIAGE

The tail hangs at rest.

During movement the tail is slightly raised and curved.

bushy-haired. At rest the tail hangs in a slight sabre-like curve; when moving it is raised with an increased curve but ideally should never be carried above the level of the back.

GAIT/MOVEMENT

KC

Sequence of step follows diagonal pattern, moving foreleg and opposite hindleg forward simultaneously; hindfoot thrust forward to midpoint of body and having equally long reach with forefeet without any noticeable change in backline. Absolute soundness of movement essential.

AKC

A German Shepherd Dog is a trotting dog, and its structure has been developed to meet the requirements of its work. *General Impression:* The gait is outreaching, elastic, seemingly without effort, smooth and rhythmic, covering the maximum amount of ground with the minimum number of steps. At a walk it covers a great deal of ground, with long stride of both hind legs and forelegs. At a trot the dog covers still more ground with even longer stride, and moves powerfully but easily, with coordination and balance so that the gait appears to be the steady motion of a well-lubricated machine. The feet travel close to the ground on both forward reach and backward push. In order to

achieve ideal movement of this kind, there must be good muscular development and ligamentation. The hindquarters deliver, through the back, a powerful forward thrust which slightly lifts the whole animal and drives the body forward. Reaching far under, and passing the imprint left by the front foot, the hind foot takes hold of the ground; then hock, stifle and upper thigh come into play and sweep back, the stroke of the hind leg finishing with the foot still close to the ground in a smooth follow-through. The overreach of the hindquarter usually necessitates one hind foot passing outside and the other hind foot passing inside

the track of the forefeet, and such action is not faulty unless the locomotion is crabwise with the dog's body sideways out of the normal straight line. *Transmission:* The typical smooth, flowing gait is maintained with great strength and firmness of back. The whole effort of the hindquarter is transmitted to the forequarter through the loin, back and withers. At full trot, the back must remain firm and level without sway, roll, whip or roach. Unlevel topline with withers lower than the hip is a fault. To compensate for the forward motion imparted by the hindquarters, the shoulder should open to its full extent.

A dog has to be built correctly in order to move soundly.

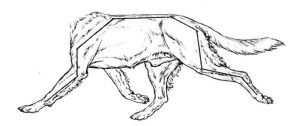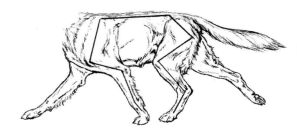

There is a considerable change in the angulation of a German Shepherd's limbs as he moves.

The forelegs should reach out close to the ground in a long stride in harmony with that of the hindquarters. The dog does not track on widely separated parallel lines, but brings the feet inward toward the middle line of the body when trotting, in order to maintain balance. The feet track closely but do not strike or cross over. Viewed from the front, the front legs function from the shoulder joint to the pad in a straight line. Viewed from the rear, the hind legs function from the hip joint to the pad in a straight line. Faults of gait, whether from front, rear or side, are to be considered very serious faults.

FCI

The German Shepherd Dog is a trotter. His gait exhibits diagonal movement, i.e., the hind foot and the forefoot on opposite sides move simultaneously.

The limbs, therefore, must be so similarly proportioned to one another, i.e. angulated, that the action of the rear as it carries through to the middle of the body and is matched by an equally far-reaching forehand causes no essential change in the topline.

Every tendency toward overangulation of the rear quarters diminishes soundness and endurance. The correct proportions of height to length and corresponding length of the leg bones results in a ground-eating gait that is low to the ground and imparts an impression of effortless progression.

With his head thrust forward and a slightly raised tail, a balanced and even trotter will have a topline that falls in moderate curves from the tip of the ears over the neck and level back through the tip of the tail.

The GSD is an endurance trotter. His sequence of steps therefore follows a diagonal pattern in that he always moves the foreleg and the opposite hindleg forward at the same time. To achieve this, his limbs must be in such balance to one another so that he can thrust the hind foot well forward to the mid point of the body and have an equally long reach with the forefoot without any noticeable change in the back line.

The correct proportion of height to corresponding length of limbs will produce a ground covering stride that travels flat over the ground, giving the impression of effortless movement.

With his head thrust forward and a slightly raised tail, a balanced and even trotter displays a flowing line running from the tip of his ears over the neck and back down to the tip of the tail.

The gait should be supple, smooth and long reaching, carrying the body forward with the minimum of up and down movement, entirely free from a stilted action.

The gait is a most important consideration in the dog's appraisal, especially in the evaluation of working breeds. Correct physical construction indicates a balanced sound gait. Anatomically incorrect dogs are rarely, if ever, capable of sound movement.

There are two types of movement assessed:
- Trotting: Sequence of steps follows a diagonal pattern, moving foreleg and opposite hindleg forward simultaneously; hind foot thrust forward to the mid point of the body and having equally long reach with forefeet without any noticeable change in backline.
- Pacing: Commonly known as ambling, this is a type of gait in which the front and hind legs on the same side move in unison with one another as a pair.

COAT

KC

Outer coat consisting of straight, hard, close-lying hair as dense as possible; thick undercoat. Hair on head, ears, front of legs, paws and toes short; on back, longer and thicker; in some males forming slight ruff. Hair longer on back of legs as far down as pasterns and stifles and forming fairly thick trousers on hindquarters. No hard and fast rule for length of hair; mole-type coats undesirable.

AKC

The ideal dog has a double coat of medium length. The outer coat should be as dense as possible, hair straight, harsh and lying close to the body. A slightly wavy outer coat, often of wiry texture, is permissible. The head, including the inner ear and foreface, and the legs and paws are covered with short hair, and the neck with longer and thicker hair. The rear of the forelegs and hind legs has somewhat longer hair extending to the pastern and hock, respectively. Faults in coat include soft, silky, too long outer coat, woolly, curly, and open coat.

FCI
The medium smooth-coated German Shepherd Dog
The outer coat should be as thick as possible. The individual hairs are straight, coarse and lying flat against the body. The coat is short on the head inclusive of the ears, the front of the legs, the feet and the toes but longer and thicker on the neck. The hair grows longer on the back of the fore- and hind legs as far down as the pastern and the hock joint, forming moderate breeching on the thighs. The length of the hair varies, and due to these differences in length, there are many intermediate forms. A too short or mole-like coat is faulty.

The long-coated German Shepherd lacks the weatherproofing of a correct coat.

The long smooth-coated German Shepherd Dog

The individual hairs are longer, not always straight and above all not lying close to the body. The coat is considerably longer inside and behind the ears, on the back of the forearm and usually in the loin area. Now and then there will be tufts in the ears and feathering from elbow to pastern. The breeching along the thigh is long and thick. The tail is bushy with slight feathering underneath. The long-smooth-coat is not as weatherproof as the medium-smooth-coat and is therefore undesirable; however, provided there is sufficient undercoat, it may be passed for breeding, as long as the breed regulations of the country allow it.

With the long-smooth-coated German Shepherd Dog, a narrow chest and narrow overstretched muzzle are frequently found.

The long-coated German Shepherd Dog

The coat is considerably longer than that of the long-smooth-coat. It is generally very soft and forms a parting along the back. The undercoat will be found in the region of the loins or will not be present at all. A long coat is greatly diminished in weatherproofing and utility and therefore is undesirable.

The gold and black colour (left), and sable (right).

The GSD coat is relatively short with an undercoat, thus making the coat waterproof. The longhaired GSD is mainly devoid of the undercoat and therefore the coat is not water resistant. The long coat is an abnormality of the Breed Standard and will be penalised if shown.

However, if you don't intend to show your dog in conformation classes, there's no reason to avoid the long-coated GSD. Long-coated GSDs can and do compete in obedience and other working disciplines.

The normal coat is dominant to the long coat, therefore we have three types of hair gene in the GSD: normal, normal but carrying the long coat gene, and long. An average 8 per cent of pups are born long-coated.

COLOUR

KC

Black or black saddle with tan, or gold to light grey markings. All black, all grey, with lighter or brown markings referred to as Sables. Nose black. Light markings on chest or very pale colour on inside of legs permissible but undesirable, as are whitish nails, red-tipped tails or wishy-washy faded colours defined as lacking in pigmentation. Blues, livers, albinos, whites (i.e. almost pure white dogs with black noses) and near whites highly undesirable. Undercoat, except in all black dogs, usually grey or fawn. Colour in itself is of secondary importance having no effect on character or fitness for work. Final colour of a young dog only ascertained when outer coat has developed.

AKC

The German Shepherd Dog varies in color, and most colors are permissible. Strong rich colors are preferred. Pale, washed-out colors and blues or livers are serious faults. A white dog must be disqualified.

FCI

Colour should be black with regular markings in brown, tan to light grey, also with a black saddle, dark sable (black cover on a grey or light brown case with corresponding lighter marks), black, uniform grey or with light or brown markings. Small white markings on the fore chest or a very light colour on the insides of the legs are permissible though not desired. The nose must be black with all coat colours. (Dogs with little or no masks, yellow or strikingly light eyes, light markings on the chest and insides of the legs, white nails and a red tip of the tail or washed out weak colours are considered lacking in pigment.) The undercoat or base hair is always light grey, with the exception of that on black dogs. The final colour of a puppy is only determined when the outer coat completely develops.

The most acceptable colour in the German Shepherd coat are black and tan. Black, created by the pigment eumelanin (black hair), varies in its degree of extension over the body, while tan, created by the pigment phaeomelanin (red hair), varies in its richness. A well-pigmented dog will show black extending over at least 50% of its body, with a strong reddish tan.

However, there are a multitude of colours, ranging from: bicolour (typically, the bicolour is a black dog with tan points, much the same as a Dobermann's markings); black, no deviation in colour – just pure black; sable, which is the original wolf colour, with a paler ground colour overlaid with a mantle of black-tipped guard hairs; black and silver; and the list can continue.

Pale pigmentation is unattractive while white markings are not desirable, although a small white spot on the chest is common. Blues and livers are also born; these are not mentioned in the Breed Standard but are classed as serious faults.

The white GSD is becoming very popular worldwide. The breeders of this colour are not adhering to the Standard in all three versions, as the white GSD is classed as a very serious fault.

FAULTS

KC

Any departure from the foregoing points should be considered a fault and the seriousness with which the fault should be regarded should be in exact proportion to its degree and its effect upon the health and welfare of the dog.

Note: Male animals should have two apparently normal testicles fully descended into the scrotum.

AKC

Disqualifications:
• Cropped or hanging ears.
• Dogs with noses not predominantly black.
• Undershot jaw.
• Docked tail.
• White dogs.
• Any dog that attempts to bite the judge.

FCI

Faults include anything that impairs working versatility, endurance and working competency, especially lack of sex characteristics and temperament traits contrary to the German Shepherd Dog such as apathy, weak nerves or over excitability, shyness; lack of vitality or willingness to work; monorchids and cryptorchids and testicles too small; a soft or flabby constitution and a lack of substance; fading pigment; blues, albinos (with complete lack of pigmentation, e.g. pink nose, etc.) and whites (near to pure white with black nose); over and under size; stunted growth; high-legged dogs and those with an overloaded fore chest; a disproportionately short, too refined or coarse build; a soft back, too steep a placement of the limbs and anything depreciating the reach and endurance of gait; a muzzle that is too short, blunt, weak, pointed or narrow and lacks strength; an over or undershot bite or any other faults of dentition, especially weak or worn teeth; a coat that is too soft, too short or too long; a lack of undercoat; hanging ears, a permanently faulty ear carriage or cropped ears; a ringed, curled or generally faulty tail set; a docked tail (stumpy) or a naturally short tail.

HAPPY AND HEALTHY

Chapter 8

The German Shepherd is a very handsome dog, with a lifespan often running into double figures, provided his needs are met. He is renowned as a brave companion and a willing, non-conditional friend. However, he will, out of necessity, rely on you for food, shelter, accident prevention and medication, to remain fully fit and healthy. There are a few genetic conditions that occur in the GSD, which will be covered in depth later in the chapter.

ROUTINE HEALTH CARE

VACCINATION
There is currently much debate over the issue of vaccination. The timing of the final part of the initial vaccination course for a puppy and the frequency of subsequent booster vaccinations are both under scrutiny. An evaluation of the relative risk for each disease plays a part, depending on the local situation.

Many owners think that the actual vaccination is the protection, believing that their puppy can go out for walks as soon as he has had the final part of the puppy vaccination course. This is not the case. The rationale behind vaccination is to stimulate the immune system into producing protective antibodies, which will be triggered if the patient is subsequently exposed to that particular disease. So, after vaccination it will be a further one or two weeks before an effective level of protection will have developed. Vaccines against viruses stimulate longer-lasting protection than those against bacteria, whose effect may only persist for a matter of months in some cases. There is also the possibility of a dog failing to mount a full immune response to

a vaccination; although the vaccine schedule may have been followed as recommended, that particular dog remains vulnerable. A dog's level of protection against rabies, as demonstrated by the antibody titre in a blood sample, is routinely tested in the UK in order to fulfil the requirements of the Pet Travel Scheme (PETS). This is not the case with other individual diseases. In order to gauge the need for booster vaccination, or to determine the effect of a course of vaccines, your veterinary surgeon will advise a protocol based upon the vaccines available, local disease prevalence, and the lifestyle of you and your dog. It is worth remembering that maintaining a fully effective level of immune protection against the disease appropriate to your locale is vital; these are serious, sometimes fatal, diseases, some of which have the potential to be passed on to

When your German Shepherd goes for a booster, the vet can give him a complete check-up.

humans (so-called zoonotic potential for transmission). This is where you will be grateful for your veterinary surgeon's own knowledge and advice.

The American Animal Hospital Association laid down guidelines at the end of 2006 for the vaccination of dogs in North America. Core diseases were defined as distemper, adenovirus, parvovirus and rabies. So-called non-core diseases were listed as kennel cough, Lyme disease and leptospirosis. The decision to vaccinate against one or more non-core diseases will be based on an individual dog's level of risk, determined on lifestyle and location in the US.

However, do remember, that

the booster visit to the veterinary surgery is not 'just' for a booster. I am regularly correcting my clients when they announce that they have 'just' brought their pet for a booster. Instead, this appointment is a chance for a full health check and evaluation of your dog. After all, we are all familiar with the adage that a human year is equivalent to seven canine years. There have been attempts, in recent times, to reset the scale, for two reasons: small breeds live longer than giant breeds, and dogs are living longer generally. I have seen dogs of 17 and 18 years of age, but to say that a dog is 119 or 126 years old is plainly meaningless. It does emphasise the fact, though, that

a dog's health can change dramatically over the course of a single year, because dogs age at a far greater rate than humans. For me, as a veterinary surgeon, the booster vaccination visit is a challenge: what can I discover about the dog's overall health and condition? For example, rotten teeth or a heart murmur can be difficult for the owner to detect. Even monitoring bodyweight year upon year is important, because bodyweight can creep up or down without an owner realising. Being overweight is unhealthy, but it may take an outsider to make an owner realise that there is a problem. Conversely, a drop in bodyweight may be the only pointer to an

Kennel cough is highly contagious and will spread through dogs that live together.

underlying problem.

The diseases against which dogs are vaccinated include:

ADENOVIRUS

Canine adenovirus 1 (CAV-1) affects the liver (hepatitis) and is seen within affected dogs as the classic 'blue eye', while CAV-2 is a cause of kennel cough (see later). Vaccines often include both canine adenoviruses.

DISTEMPER

This is also called 'hardpad' from the characteristic changes to the pads of the paws. It has a worldwide distribution, but fortunately vaccination has been very effective at reducing its occurrence. It is caused by a virus

and affects the respiratory, gastro-intestinal (gut) and nervous systems, so it causes a wide range of illnesses. Fox and urban, stray dog populations are most at risk, and therefore responsible for local outbreaks.

KENNEL COUGH (INFECTIOUS TRACHEOBRONCHITIS)

Bordetella bronchiseptica is not only a major cause of kennel cough, but it is also a common secondary infection, on top of another cause. Being a bacterium, it is treatable with appropriate antibiotics, but the immunity stimulated by the vaccine is therefore short-lived (six to 12 months). This vaccine is often in

a form to be administered down the nostrils, in order to stimulate local immunity at the point of entry. Do not be alarmed if you see your vet using a needle and syringe to draw up the vaccine, because the needle will be replaced with a special plastic introducer, allowing the vaccine to be gently instilled into each nostril. Dogs generally resent being held more than the actual intra-nasal vaccine. I have learnt that covering the patient's eyes helps greatly.

Kennel cough, is rather a catch-all term for any cough spreading within a dog population, not just in kennels, but also between dogs at a training session, breed show, or even mixing out in the park.

Many of these infections may not be B. bronchiseptica but other viruses, which can only be treated symptomatically. Parainfluenza virus is often included in a vaccine programme because it is a common viral cause of kennel cough.

Kennel cough can seem alarming. There is a persistent cough, accompanied by white frothy spittle, which can last for a matter of weeks, during which time the patient is highly infectious to other dogs. I remember when it ran through my five Border Collies; there were white patches of froth on the floor wherever you looked! Other features include sneezing, a runny nose, and eyes sore with conjunctivitis. Fortunately, these infections are generally self-limiting, and most dogs recover without any long-lasting problems. However, an elderly dog may be knocked sideways by it, akin to the effects of a common cold on a frail, elderly person.

LYME DISEASE

This is a bacterial infection transmitted by hard ticks. It is found in those specific areas of the US where ticks are found, such as the north-eastern states, some southern states, California, and the upper Mississippi region.

LEPTOSPIROSIS

Leptospirosis, also known as Weil's disease in humans, is commonly contracted through contact with rats and their urine. This is a zoonotic disease, with implications for all those in contact with an affected dog. The UK National Rodent Survey 2003 found a wild, brown rat population of 60 million, equivalent at the time to one rat per person. I have heard it said that in the UK you are never more than a foot (30 cm) from a rat! This means that there is as much risk for the GSD living on the edge of a town, as there is for the GSD living in the countryside.

The situation in the US is less clear-cut. Blanket vaccination against leptospirosis is not considered necessary, because it only occurs in certain areas, so you must be guided by your vet.

It does occur in the UK as well, but at a low level, so vaccination is not routinely offered.

The clinical disease is manifested primarily as limping, due to arthritis, but other organs affected include the heart, kidneys and nervous system. It is readily treatable with appropriate antibiotics, once diagnosed, but the causal bacterium, Borrelia burgdorferi, will remain persistently within the body. Prevention requires both vaccination and tick control, especially as there are other diseases transmitted by ticks. Ticks carrying B. burgdorferi will transmit it to humans as well, but

an infected dog cannot pass it to a human.

PARVOVIRUS

This appeared in the late 1970s, when it was thought that the UK's dog population would be decimated by it. While this was a terrifying possibility at the time, it fortunately did not happen on the scale envisaged. Occurrence is mainly low now, thanks to vaccination. It is occasionally seen in the elderly unvaccinated dog.

RABIES

This is another zoonotic disease, and there are very strict control measures in place. Vaccines were once only available in the UK, on an individual basis for dogs being taken abroad. Pets travelling into the UK had to serve six months' compulsory quarantine so that any pet incubating rabies would be identified before being released back into the general population. Under the Pet Travel Scheme, provided certain criteria are met (refer to the DEFRA website for up-to-date information – www.defra.gov.uk), then dogs can re-enter the UK without being quarantined. Dogs being imported into the US have to show that they were vaccinated against rabies at least 30 days before travelling;

otherwise, they have to serve effective internal quarantine for 30 days from the date of vaccination to ensure they are not incubating rabies. The exception is dogs entering from countries recognised as being rabies-free, in which case it has to be proved that they lived in that country for at least six months beforehand.

PARASITES

A parasite is defined as an organism deriving benefit, on a one-way basis, from another – the host. It goes without saying that it is not to the parasite's advantage to harm the host to such an extent that the benefit is lost, especially if it results in the death of the host. This means a dog could harbour parasites,

internal and/or external, without there being any signs apparent to the owner. Many canine parasites can, however, transfer to humans with variable consequences, so routine preventative treatment is advised against particular parasites. Just as with vaccination, risk assessment plays a part. For example, there is no need for routine heartworm treatment in the UK (at present), but it is vital in the US and in Mediterranean countries.

INTERNAL PARASITES
ROUNDWORMS
(NEMATODES)

These are the spaghetti-like worms that you may have been unfortunate enough to have seen passed in faeces or brought up in

vomit. Most of the deworming treatments in use today cause the adult roundworms to disintegrate, so treating puppies, in particular, is not as unpleasant as it used to be! Most puppies will have a worm burden, mainly of a particular roundworm species (Toxocara canis), which reactivates within the dam's tissues during pregnancy and passes to the foetuses developing in the womb. It is therefore important to treat the dam both during and after pregnancy, as well as the puppies.

Professional advice is to continue worming every month. There are roundworm eggs in the environment, and, unless you examine your dog's faeces under a microscope on a very regular

The breeder will start a worming programme, which you will need to continue.

basis for the presence of roundworm eggs, you will be unaware of your dog having picked up roundworms, unless he should have such a heavy burden that he passes the adults. It takes a few weeks from the time that a dog swallows a Toxocara canis roundworm egg to him passing viable eggs (the pre-patent period). There are deworming products that are active all the time, which will provide continuous protection when administered as often as directed. Otherwise, treating every month will prevent your dog becoming a source of roundworm eggs to the general population. It is the risk to human health that is so important: T. canis roundworms will migrate within our tissues and cause all manner of problems, not least of which is blindness. If a dog has roundworms, the eggs also find their way on to his coat, where they can be picked up during stroking and cuddling. You should always carefully pick up your dog's faeces and dispose of them appropriately. This will not only reduce the chance for environmental contamination, but it will also make walking more pleasant underfoot.

TAPEWORMS (CESTODES)

When considering the general dog population, the primary source of the most common tapeworm species will be fleas, which can carry the eggs. Most multi-wormers will be active against these tapeworms – not because they are a hazard to human health, but because it is unpleasant to see the wriggly rice grain tapeworm segments emerging from your dog's back passage while he is lying in front of the fire, and usually when you have guests for dinner.

There are specific requirements for treatment with praziquantel within 24 to 48 hours of returning to the UK under PETS. This is to prevent the inadvertent introduction of Echinococcus multilocularis, a tapeworm carried by foxes on mainland Europe, which is transmissible to humans, causing serious or even fatal liver disease.

HEARTWORM (DIROFILARIA IMMITIS)

Heartworm infection has been diagnosed in dogs all over the world. There are two prerequisites: the presence of mosquitoes and a warm humid climate. When a female mosquito bites an infected animal, it acquires D. immitis in its circulating form as microfilariae. A warm environmental temperature is needed for these microfilariae to develop into the infective third-stage larvae (L3) within the mosquitoes, the so-called intermediate host. L3 larvae are then transmitted by the mosquito when it next bites a dog. Therefore, while heartworm infection is found in all the states of the US, it is at such differing levels, that an occurrence in Alaska, for example, is probably a reflection of a visiting dog having previously picked up the infection elsewhere.

Heartworm infection is not currently a problem in the UK, except for those dogs contracting it while abroad without suitable preventative treatment. However, global warming, and its effect on the UK's climate, could change that. It is a potentially life-threatening condition, with dogs of all breeds and ages being susceptible without preventative treatment. The larvae can grow to 14 inches within the right side of the heart, causing primarily signs of heart failure, and ultimately, liver and kidney damage. It can be treated, but prevention is a better plan. In the US, regular blood tests for the presence of infection are advised, coupled with appropriate preventative measures, so liaison with your vet is advised. For dogs travelling to heartworm-endemic areas of the EU, such as

To date, heartworm is not a problem for dogs living in the UK.

the Mediterranean coast, preventative treatment should be started before leaving the UK and maintained during the visit. Again, this is best arranged with your vet.

EXTERNAL PARASITES

FLEAS
There are several species of flea, which are not host-specific. Not only can a dog be carrying cat and human fleas, as well as dog fleas, but the same flea treatment will kill and/or control them all. It is also accepted that environmental control is a vital part of a flea control programme. This is because the adult flea is only on the animal for as long as it takes to have a blood meal and to breed; the remainder of the life cycle occurs in the house, car, caravan, shed etc. There is a vast array of flea control products available, with various routes of administration: collar, powder, spray, 'spot-on', and oral. Since flea control needs to be applied to all pets in the house, independent of whether they leave the house or not, it is best to discuss your specific flea-control needs with your vet.

TICKS
There were once said to be classic pockets of ticks in the UK, such as the New Forest and Thetford Forest, but they are actually found nationwide. The life cycle is curious; each life stage takes a

year to develop, and move on to the next. Long grass is a major habitat; the vibration of animals moving through the grass will stimulate the larva, nymph or adult to climb up a blade of grass and wave its legs in the air as it 'quests' for a host to latch on to for its next blood meal. Humans are just as likely to be hosts as dogs, so ramblers and orienteers are advised to cover their legs when going through rough long grass. As well as their physical presence causing irritation, it is the potential for disease transmission that is of most concern. A tick will transmit any infection previously contracted while feeding on an animal – for example, Borrelia burgdorferi, the causal agent of Lyme disease (see page 134).

A-Z OF COMMON AILMENTS

ACUTE MOIST DERMATITIS (AMD) OR HOT SPOT

This is often seen in the young GSD, either just below the ear or on the rump. The skin and overlying fur appear wet, which is due to a sticky discharge caused by the infection in the skin. The area is very painful to the touch, so it is often necessary to sedate the patient before clipping away the fur. A large area of infected skin may be revealed, but removing the fur back to visually, healthy skin enables a thorough cleansing of the affected area. A course of appropriate oral antibiotics is often prescribed, together with topical treatment. The response is generally rapid,

the infection resolving within ten to fourteen days.

The initial cause may have been an insect sting, or an ear infection (see below) stimulating the dog to scratch his ear, and thereby irritating the skin below it. Patient interference does play a role in the development of AMD; a vicious cycle is established because the infected area is itchy for the dog. Preventing further scratching and rubbing of the area is paramount, in order for the infection to clear up.

ANAL SACS, IMPACTED

The anal sacs lie on either side of the back passage or anus, at approximately four and eight o'clock, if compared with the face of a clock. They fill with a particularly pungent fluid, which

We need to be aware of the dangers of tick-borne disease – particularly for dogs that live in the country.

is emptied on to the faeces as they move past the sacs to exit from the anus. Theories abound as to why these sacs should become impacted periodically, and seemingly more so in some dogs than others. The irritation of impacted anal sacs is often seen as 'scooting', when the backside is dragged along the ground. Some dogs will also gnaw at their back feet or over the rump.

Increasing the fibre content of the diet helps some dogs, although in others, there may be an underlying skin disease. It may be a one-off occurrence, for no apparent reason. Sometimes, an infection can become established, requiring antibiotic therapy, which may need to be coupled with flushing out the infected sac under sedation or general anaesthesia. More rarely, a dog will present with an apparently acute-onset anal sac abscess, which is incredibly painful.

DIARRHOEA

The cause and treatment is much as Gastritis (see below).

FOREIGN BODIES (INTERNAL)

Items swallowed in haste, without checking whether they

EAR INFECTIONS

Dogs have a long external ear canal, initially vertical then horizontal, leading to the eardrum, which protects the middle ear. If your GSD is shaking his head, then his ears will need to be inspected with an auroscope by your vet, to identify any cause and to ensure the eardrum is intact. A sample may be taken from the canal, to be examined under the microscope and cultured to identify causal agents. The vet will then prescribe appropriate eardrops containing antibiotic, anti-fungal agent and/or steroid. Predisposing causes of otitis externa or infection in the external ear canal include: presence of a foreign body (such as a grass awn); ear mites, which are intensely irritating to the dog and stimulate the production of brown wax, predisposing to infection; previous infections, causing the canal's lining to thicken, narrowing the canal and reducing ventilation; and swimming – some GSDs love swimming, but water trapped in the external ear canal can lead to infection, especially if the water is not clean.

can be digested, can cause problems if they lodge in the stomach or obstruct the intestines, necessitating surgical removal. Acute vomiting is the main indication. Common objects I have seen removed include stones from the garden, peach stones, babies' dummies, golf balls, and once, a lady's bra! It is possible to diagnose a dog with an intestinal obstruction across a waiting room, from a particularly 'tucked-up' stance

and pained facial expression. These dogs bounce back from surgery dramatically. A previously docile and compliant obstructed patient will return for a post-operative check-up and literally bounce into the consulting room.

EXTERNAL

Grass awns are adept at finding their way into orifices such as a nostril, down an ear, and into the soft skin between two digits (toes), where they start a one-way journey, due to the direction of their whiskers. In particular, I remember a grass awn that migrated from a hind paw, causing abscesses along the way but not yielding itself up until it erupted through the skin in the groin.

GASTRITIS

This is usually a simple stomach upset, most commonly in response to dietary indiscretion. Scavenging constitutes a change in the diet as much as an abrupt switch in the food given by the owner. Generally, a day without food, followed by a few days of small, frequent meals of a bland diet (such as cooked chicken or fish) or an appropriate prescription diet, should allow the stomach to settle. It is vital to

Beware of the danger of grass awns if your dog exercises in long grass.

wean the patient back on to routine food or else another bout of gastritis may occur.

JOINT PROBLEMS

It is not unusual for the older GSD to be stiff after exercise, particularly in cold weather. This is not really surprising, given that the GSD is a breed with a big frame. Your veterinary surgeon will be able to advise you on ways to help your dog cope with stiffness, such as ensuring that he is not overweight. Arthritic joints do not need to be burdened with extra bodyweight!

LUMPS

Regularly handling and stroking your dog will enable the early detection of any lumps or bumps. These may be due to

infection (abscess), bruising, multiplication of particular cells within the body, or even an external parasite (tick). If you are worried about any lump you find, have it checked by your vet.

OBESITY

Being overweight predisposes the German Shepherd to many other problems, such as diabetes mellitus, heart disease and joint problems. It is so easily prevented by simply acting as your Shepherd's conscience. Ignore pleading eyes, and feed according to your dog's waistline. The body condition is what matters qualitatively, alongside monitoring the dog's bodyweight as a quantitative measure. The German Shepherd should have at least a suggestion of a waist, and

it should be possible to feel the ribs beneath only a slight layer of fat.

Neutering does not automatically mean that your German Shepherd will be overweight. Having an ovario-hysterectomy does slow down the body's metabolic rate, castration to a lesser extent. This therefore means that your dog needs less food. I recommend cutting back a little on the amount of food fed a few weeks before neutering, to accustom your Shepherd to less food. If the dog looks very slightly underweight on the morning of the operation, it will help the veterinary surgeon as well as giving the dog a little leeway weight-wise afterwards. It is always harder to lose weight after neutering than before, because of this slowing in the body's inherent metabolic rate.

TEETH

In the wild, dogs eat by gripping and killing prey with the canine teeth – biting off pieces of food with the incisors and chewing it with the molars. To be able to eat is vital for life, yet the actual health of the teeth is often overlooked. Unhealthy teeth can predispose a dog to disease, and not just by reducing the ability to eat. The presence of infection within the mouth can lead to bacteria entering the bloodstream and then filtering out at major organs, with the potential for serious consequences. That is not to forget that simply having dental pain can affect a dog's well-being, as anyone who has

Regular exercise will help to keep your German Shepherd lean and healthy.

had toothache will confirm. Veterinary dentistry has made huge leaps in recent years, so that it no longer consists of extraction as the treatment of necessity.

Good dental health lies in the hands of the owner, starting from the moment the dog comes into your care. Just as we have taken on responsibility for feeding, we have also acquired the task of maintaining good dental and oral hygiene. In an ideal world, we should brush our dogs' teeth as regularly as our own. The German Shepherd puppy who finds having his teeth brushed a huge game and excuse to roll over and over on the ground requires loads of patience, twice a day.

There are alternative strategies, ranging from dental chewsticks to specially formulated foods, but the main thing is to be aware of your dog's mouth. At least train your puppy to permit full examination of his teeth, which will not only ensure you are checking in his mouth regularly, but will also make your vet's job easier when there is a real need for your dog to 'open wide!'

INHERITED DISORDERS

Any individual, dog or human, may have an inherited disorder, by virtue of genes acquired from their parents. This is significant, not only for the health of that individual but also because of the potential for transmitting the disorder on to their offspring and to subsequent generations, depending on the mode of inheritance.

There are control schemes in place for some inherited disorders. In the US, for example, the Canine Eye Registration Foundation (CERF) was set up by dog breeders concerned about heritable eye disease. It provides a database of dogs who have been examined by diplomats of the American College of Veterinary Ophthalmologists.

There are several major disorders that are thought to be inherited in the German Shepherd Dog:

ANAL FURUNCULOUS

This is an extensive tract formation, deep into the tissue around the anus, often spreading quite some distance away. The cause is unknown. A secondary bacterial infection is not

There are a number of inherited disorders within the breed, which is why all breeding stock must be screened.

uncommon, so that it will often improve with antibiotic treatment. Research has shown that the tracts do not originate from the intestinal tract or the anal sacs. The tail carriage of the German Shepherd has been blamed, with the tail being held close to the perianal area, preventing good ventilation of the area. The result looks horrific, with the area around the anus laid open and weeping. An owner may be unaware of it developing, because the pain makes an affected dog becomes very wary of allowing an examination of the rear end. I particularly remember one owner who came to see me in floods of tears because she had just discovered this large raw area under her Shepherd's tail. She was blaming herself for failing to find it sooner and for being in some way responsible. It is, however, a condition that seemingly manifests very quickly, and it is probably innate in an individual GSD, due to a fault in the immune system, which may be hereditary.

It tends to occur initially in middle-aged dogs. Various treatments have been tried, both surgical and medical, with varying degrees of success, which may reflect individual differences in the condition. Recurrence is a further problem.

AORTIC STENOSIS

This is a congenital malformation of the major outflow vessel from the heart, i.e. present at birth.

CATARACT, HEREDITARY

In the German Shepherd this shows an autosomal recessive pattern of inheritance. A cataract is a cloudiness of the lens of the eye. In German Shepherds, this is the early-onset form of hereditary cataract, starting at eight to 12 weeks of age in the posterior sutures of the lens. It is slowly progressive, and controlled under Schedule A of the BVA/KC/ISDS Scheme** in the UK, CERF in the US.

142

Excessive exercise while a puppy is growing can contribute to joint problems.

ELBOW DYSPLASIA

In the German Shepherd, the anconeal and medial coronoid processes are commonly affected. Although occurrence within the breed seems to be rising, this could be a reflection of increased use, by breeders, of screening under the BVA/KC Scheme*. Standard radiographs of both elbows can be taken once an individual has passed his first birthday, and each elbow is scored from zero (unaffected) through to 3 (worst). The highest score of the two elbows is given as that dog's score, with breeders being advised to breed only from those with scores of zero or one. Each dog can only have his elbows scored once in a lifetime.

EPILEPSY

This is often called juvenile epilepsy, because it manifests in the immature and young adult GSD (six months to three years old), with convulsions occurring singly or in clusters. It is very alarming, as an owner, to see your dog having a fit, because you feel utterly helpless. It is vital to note when a fit, or cluster of fits, occurs together with information about concurrent happenings (for example, family gathering,

television switched on, fireworks, middle of the night). Even if a young adult German Shepherd came to see me having had just one fit, I would be unlikely to start medication at once, because 'every dog is allowed one or two fits'. Once medication has started, it is impossible to assess whether or not the dog would have continued fitting. If it is needed to control the fits, then medication will, from the nature of the problem, be life-long.

HIP DYSPLASIA

This is a malformation of the hip joints, causing pain, lameness and reduced exercise tolerance in the young German Shepherd Dog, resulting in degenerative joint disease (arthritis) in the older dog. Each hip joint is scored on several features to give a total of zero to 53 from a radiograph taken with the hips and pelvis in a specified position, usually requiring the dog to be sedated, after the age of one, under the BVA/KC Scheme*, from two years of age in the US (OFA***).

MITRAL DYSPLASIA

This is a congenital malformation of the mitral valve of the heart, which lies between the left atrium and left ventricle. Inheritance is suspected, with a predisposition for the male. It is often detected at a puppy's first health check as a murmur on the left-hand side of the chest. The effects of the leaky valve are variable and relate to the damming back of blood to the lungs, primarily causing a cough. Radiography and ultrasound examination are the mainstays of diagnosis and also help in tracking progression of the affected GSD's condition. Although this malformation cannot be cured, it can be managed with appropriate medication (see also Tricuspid valve dysplasia).

TRICUSPID VALVE DYSPLASIA (TVD)

This is another congenital heart defect. An affected individual is born with a malformed heart valve, between the two chambers of the right side of the heart. The heart's ability to act as a pump depends on the integrity of its valves. A wide spectrum of effect is seen, ranging from a slight malformation having little effect on the dog's life span, to such a leaky valve that congestive heart failure develops while young. Blood leaking back through the valve causes turbulence in the blood flow, and the normally clear click as the valve closes is muffled. This is heard as a murmur when a stethoscope is placed on the chest wall, especially over the valve. A common time to first suspect TVD is when a veterinary surgeon examines the puppy at a first health check or prior to starting a vaccination course. A detailed ultrasound examination is needed to diagnose and stage the extent of the problem.

PANNUS

The textbook name of chronic superficial keratitis describes this condition, namely as a long-term inflammation of the cornea. There is often a conjunctivitis or inflammation of the conjunctiva as well. Inheritance is recessive in nature, but with variation in the extent of the inflammation between affected individuals. Ultimately, blindness can result.

Treatment is more of a management consideration, in an attempt to limit the effects and progression of the inflammation.

Exposure to ultraviolet lightwaves may play a role; minimising time spent in full sun is also advised, keeping exercise to the early morning or evening.

PITUITARY DWARFISM

Unlike achondroplastic dwarves, where there is an alteration in bodily proportions, the adult pituitary dwarf German Shepherd Dog is perfectly shaped but simply much smaller than the normal adult. It is therefore vital to remember that adult pituitary dwarves are adults imprisoned within undersized bodies. They not only require the respect one would accord an adult but will also age like an adult.

An affected puppy first becomes apparent at two to three months of age, as his size falls behind his littermates. The puppy fur may not be replaced with the adult coat, reflecting an underactive thyroid gland. Supplementation with thyroid hormone will prevent this to some degree.

The pituitary dwarf I knew was a real character. He grew no bigger than the size of an English Springer Spaniel but behaved as if he were a big German Shepherd. Despite various health problems,

Increasingly, owners are becoming aware of the benefit of complementary therapies.

including one episode of gastric dilatation volvulus, he lived to 10 years of age.

*British Veterinary Association/Kennel Club Scheme
** British Veterinary Association/Kennel Club/International Sheepdog Society Scheme
***Orthopedic Foundation for Animals, US

COMPLEMENTARY THERAPIES

Just as for human health, there is a place for alternative therapies, but alongside and complementing orthodox treatment, under the supervision of a veterinary surgeon. This is why 'complementary therapies' is a more appropriate name than 'alternative therapies'. Because animals do not have a choice, there are measures in place to safeguard their well-being and welfare. All manipulative treatment must be under the direction of a veterinary surgeon, who has examined the patient and diagnosed the condition that they feel needs that form of treatment. This covers physiotherapy, chiropractic, osteopathy and swimming therapy. For example, dogs with arthritis who cannot exercise as freely as they were once

accustomed to will enjoy the sensation of controlled non-weight-bearing exercise in water. This will also improve their muscles and overall fitness.

All other complementary therapies, such as acupuncture, homoeopathy and aromatherapy, can only be carried out by veterinary surgeons trained in that particular field.

ACUPUNCTURE
This is mainly used in pain relief, often to good effect. The needles look more alarming to the owner, but they are very fine and are well tolerated by most canine patients. Speaking personally,

superficial needling is not unpleasant and does help with pain relief.

HOMOEOPATHY

This has had a mixed press in recent years. It is based on the concept of treating like with like. Additionally, a homoeopathic remedy is said to become more powerful the more it is diluted.

SUMMARY

As the owner of a German Shepherd, you are responsible for his care and health. Not only must you make decisions on his behalf, you are also responsible for establishing a lifestyle for him, which will ensure he leads a long and happy life.

Diet plays an important part in this, as does exercise. For example, nutritional manipulation has a long history. For the domestic dog, it is only in recent years that the need has been recognised for changing the diet to suit the dog as he grows, matures, and then enters his

With good care and management, your German Shepherd should live a long, happy and healthy life.

twilight years. So-called life-stage diets try to match the nutritional needs of the dog as he progresses through life. An adult dog food will suit the German Shepherd living a standard family life. There are also foods for those Shepherds tactfully termed as 'obese-prone', such as those who have been neutered,

are less active than others, or just simply like their food. Do remember, though, that ultimately you are in control of your German Shepherd's diet, unless he is able to profit from scavenging! On the other hand, prescription diets are of necessity fed under the supervision of a veterinary surgeon, because each is formulated to meet the very specific needs of a particular health condition. Should a prescription diet be fed to a healthy dog, or to a dog with a different illness, there could be adverse effects.

It is important to remember that your German Shepherd has no choice. As his owner, you are responsible for any decision made, so it must be as informed as possible. Always speak to your vet if you have any worries about your GSD. He is not just a dog, because he will become a definite member of the family from the moment you bring him home.

THE CONTRIBUTORS

THE EDITOR
ANDREW WINFROW (Sadira)

It was 42 years ago that Andrew handled his first German Shepherd Dog, Alasyn Skillian Javelin; this male went on to produce his family's first Champion in 1976 with Ch. Sadira Francine. Although only a small kennel, Sadira has been honoured with the Top Female winning GSD title in 1976, 1980, 1999, 2000 and 2001 having bred or owned five UK Champions.

As an International Championship show judge, Andrew has had the pleasure of judging this noble breed at Crufts and around the world. He is currently an assessor for the Kennel Club in Conformation and Movement and Hand On Assessment Breed Council Surveyor. For the past four years, Andrew has been a United Kingdom delegate representing the German Shepherd Dog at the main WUSV meeting in Germany.
See Chapter Seven: The Perfect German Shepherd Dog.

GILL WARD (Belezra)

Gill's lifetime involvement with German Shepherd Dogs began during childhood. Her mother had a very successful kennel, training, showing and breeding German Shepherds, and Gill grew up with a deep love and understanding of the breed.

Gill developed a particular interest in training, and she is now a qualified training instructor for the British Association for German Shepherds Dogs. She has judged the breed at Open conformation shows and has trained and qualified her own dogs in the sport of VPG (Schutzhund).

At present, Gill is Head Instructor at a branch of the British Association for German Shepherd Dogs in Cornwall, helping pet owners to understand and cope with the family German Shepherd in all situations, training their dogs using motivation and reward techniques. Together with her husband, John, she owns a successful German Shepherd Dog kennel with the affix Belezra. Over the years, they have owned two Champions in the breed, won CCs and reserve CCs, and imported dogs from Germany.
See Chapter One: Getting to Know the German Shepherd Dog.

DOROTHY CULLUM (Cermar)

Dorothy was first introduced to the German Shepherd Dog in 1971. Her success in the world of horses made her keen to train her dog, which won for her in the breed, obedience and trials sports. She later purchased another Shepherd, accomplishing the same with her, and eventually bred from both and registered her affix Cermar.

Dorothy has judged all three sports, becoming a Championship Obedience judge, and has trained with many of the great names. She was elected on to the GSD League Committee in 1989 and for a short time was chairman. She was invited to be a member of the LKA in 1990, and an affiliate member of the Kennel Club in 2007. She ran the National Training programme with John Cree, starting the North v South obedience matches held annually at the Chamionship Show.

Dorothy is a founder member of both the KC Accredited Breeder, and KC Accredited Trainers Scheme, and tests for the KC Good Citizen Schemes.
See Chapter Two: The First German Shepherds.

JOHN WARD (Belezra)

John has been involved in German Shepherds since 1969, registering the affix of Belezra in 1970. He is an international Championship show judge of German Shepherds, GSD Breed Council Surveyor, an executive member of the British Association of German Shepherd Dogs, and currently event manager of the British Sieger.
See Chapter Two: The First German Shepherds.

KATRINA STEVENS (Kesyra)

Katrina bought her first German Shepherd Dog in 1975, which she worked in obedience and has been closely involved with the breed ever since. Over the years, she has worked as an obedience instructor and has assessed dogs for the Kennel Club Good Citizen test.

She registered her affix Kesyra and bred her first litter in 1985. She is dedicated to producing sound, healthy dogs of good character. Katrina qualified under the GSD League to judge the breed in 1988 and has herself enjoyed reasonable success in the show ring, having bred Championship and Best of Breed winners. She has served on the committee of the South Western GSD club and the German Shepherd League of Great Britain. Katrina is also the author of *The German Shepherd Dog – Breed Basics*, a book specifically written for the German Shepherd pet owner.
See Chapter Three: A German Shepherd for your Lifestyle.

JAN RALPH (Bonvivant)

Dogs have been part of Jan's life since childhood. She is interested in all aspects of dogdom, dating back to her days in Young Farmers when she was involved with livestock judging. She was also trained in horsemanship, with an emphasis on conformation, training, behaviour and breeding. Much of what she has learnt has stood her in good stead in understanding dogs, especially the formative period of puppies, and the problems with rescued dogs.

Jan is a keen photographer of dogs, and has interests in showing, agility, obedience and working trials. She has also been involved with running puppy socialisation and training classes. She judges German Shepherds and Pembroke Corgis at Open show level, and award CCs in Belgian Shepherds.

Jan shows dogs both in the UK and overseas, and has a special interest in breed history and bloodlines.
See Chapter Four: The New Arrival.

GARY GRAY (Slatehouse)

Gary has been around dogs all his life. He handled his first dog when he was eight, which, in truth, dragged him around the ring until it was tired. His love affair with the German Shepherd Dog began aged 11, when he became involved in obedience and showing dogs as a junior handler. Since then, Gary has piloted nine UK show Champions to their respective titles, three of which he has owned. The most famous representative from the Slatehouse kennel was the multiple Group-winning Ch. Norwulf Going for Gold of Slatehouse, who became the top Group-winning GSD of all time.

As a handler, Gary has amassed 50 Challenge Certificates to date. He is a member of the Kennel Club and serves on the committee of Windsor Championship Dog Show, and has served on several GSD and general canine societies. Gary judges GSDs at Championship show level, and judges most breeds at in the Working and Pastoral Groups at Open level. He has also judged at the Junior Handling Association semi-finals on two occasions.
See Chapter Five: The Best of Care.

JULIA BARNES

Julia has owned and trained a number of different dog breeds, and is a puppy socialiser for Dogs for the Disabled. A former journalist, she has written many books, including several on dog training and behaviour. Julia is indebted to Katrina Stevens (Kesyra) for help with this chapter.
See Chapter Six: Training and Socialisation.

ALISON LOGAN MA VetMB MRCVS

Alison qualified as a veterinary surgeon from Cambridge University in 1989, having been brought up surrounded by all manner of animals and birds in the north Essex countryside. She has been in practice in her home town ever since, living with her husband, two children and Labrador Retriever Pippin.

She contributes on a regular basis to *Veterinary Times, Veterinary Nurse Times, Dogs Today, Cat World* and *Pet Patter,* the PetPlan newsletter. In 1995, Alison won the Univet Literary Award with an article on Cushing's Disease, and she won it again (as the Vetoquinol Literary Award) in 2002, writing about common conditions in the Shar-Pei.
See Chapter Eight: Happy and Healthy.

USEFUL ADDRESSES

BREED CLUBS

Birmingham and district GSD Association
www.birminghamanddistrictgsd.co.uk

Bolton and District GSD Club
www.boltongsd.com

GSD Club of Northern Ireland
www.germanshepherdclubofni.com

GSD Club of Wales
www.gsdwales.co.uk

GSD League of Great Britain
www.gsdleague.co.uk

Heads of the Valleys GSD Club
www.headsvalleygsdclub.co.uk

Iceni GSD Club
www.icenigsdclub.mysite.wanadoo-members.co.uk

Midland Counties GSD Association
www.mcgsdda.co.uk

Norfolk GSD Club
www.norfolk.gsd.co.uk

North Eastern GSD Club
www.bgeocities.com/Heartland/Hills/9623/negsdc.html

Sheffield GSD Society
www.sheffieldgsd.com

Tyne Valley GSD Club
www.germanshepherd.org.uk

West Yorkshire GSD Club
www.westyorkshiregsdclub.co.uk

Other Breed Clubs
To obtain up-to-date contact information for any of the following breed clubs, which do not have websites, please contact the Kennel Club.

- Allerton GSD Club
- British Association for GSDs (operates regional branches)
- Clyde Valley GSD Club
- Crewe and North Staffs GSD Club
- Derbyshire GSD Club
- Fife GSD Club
- GSD Club of the United Kingdom
- GSD Club of Bristol
- GSD Club of Devon
- GSD Club of Essex
- GSD Club of Hertfordshire
- GSD Club Kent
- GSD Club of Scotland
- GSD Club of Suffolk
- Grampion GSD Association
- Humberside GSD Club
- Leicestershire GSD Club
- North Wales Alsatian Club
- North Yorkshire and South Durham GSD Club
- Preston and Fylde GSD Club
- South Western GSD Club
- South Yorkshire Alsatian Association
- Southern German Shepherd Dog Club

KENNEL CLUBS

American Kennel Club (AKC)
5580 Centerview Drive
Raleigh, NC 27606
Telephone: 919 233 9767
Fax: 919 233 3627
Email: info@akc.org
Web: www.akc.org

The Kennel Club (UK)
1 Clarges Street
London, W1J 8AB
Telephone: 0870 606 6750
Fax: 0207 518 1058
Web: www.the-kennel-club.org.uk

TRAINING AND BEHAVIOUR

Association of Pet Dog Trainers
PO Box 17
Kempsford, GL7 4W7
Telephone: 01285 810811
Email: APDToffice@aol.com
Web: http://www.apdt.co.uk

Association of Pet Behaviour Counsellors
PO BOX 46
Worcester, WR8 9YS
Telephone: 01386 751151
Fax: 01386 750743
Email: info@apbc.org.uk
Web: http://www.apbc.org.uk/

ACTIVITIES

Agility Club
http://www.agilityclub.co.uk/

British Flyball Association
PO Box 109, Petersfield, GU32 1XZ
Telephone: 01753 620110
Fax: 01726 861079
Email: bfa@flyball.org.uk
Web: http://www.flyball.org.uk/

Schutzhund
Contact GSDL of Great Brtain.

Working Trials
36 Elwyndene Road, March, Cambridgeshire, PE15 9RL.
www.workingtrials.co.uk

World Canine Freestyle Organisation
P.O. Box 350122, Brooklyn, NY 11235-2525, USA
Telephone: (718) 332-8336
Fax: (718) 646-2686
Email: wcfodogs@aol.com
Web: www.worldcaninefreestyle.org

HEALTH

Alternative Veterinary Medicine Centre
Chinham House, Stanford in the Vale, Oxfordshire, SN7 8NQ
Email: enquiries@bahvs.com
Web: www.bahvs.com

British Association of Veterinary Ophthalmologists (BAVO)
Email: hjf@vetspecialists.co.uk or secretary@bravo.org.uk
Web: http://www.bravo.org.uk/

British Small Animal Veterinary Association
Woodrow House, 1 Telford Way, Waterwells Business Park, Quedgeley, Gloucestershire, GL2 2AB
Telephone: 01452 726700
Fax: 01452 726701
Email: customerservices@bsava.com
Web: http://www.bsava.com/

British Veterinary Hospitals Association
Station Bungalow, Main Rd, Stocksfield, Northumberland, NE43 7HJ
Telephone: 07966 901619
Fax: 07813 915954
Email: office@bvha.org.uk
Web: http://www.bvha.org.uk/

Royal College of Veterinary Surgeons (RCVS)
Belgravia House, 62-64 Horseferry Road, London, SW1P 2AF
Telephone: 0207 222 2001
Fax: 0207 222 2004
Email: admin@rcvs.org.uk
Web: www.rcvs.org.uk

ASSISTANCE DOGS

Canine Partners for Independence,
Mill Lane, Heyshott, Midhurst, West Sussex, GU29 0ED
Telephone: 08456 580480
www.caninepartners.co.uk

Dogs for the Disabled
The Frances Hay Centre, Blacklocks Hill Banbury, Oxon, OX17 2BS
Telephone: 01295 252600
Web: www.dogsforthedisabled.org

Guide Dogs for the Blind Association
Burghfield Common, Reading, RG7 3YG
Telephone: 01189 835555
Web: www.guidedogs.org.uk/

Hearing Dogs for Deaf People
The Grange, Wycombe Road, Saunderton, Princes Risborough, Bucks, HP27 9NS
Telephone: 01844 348100
Web: hearingdogs.org.uk

Pets as Therapy
3 Grange Farm Cottages, Wycombe Road, Saunderton, Princes Risborough, Bucks, HP27 9NS
Telephone: 0870 977 0003
Web: http://www.petsastherapy.org/

Support Dogs
21 Jessops Riverside, Brightside Lane, Sheffield, S9 2RX
Tel: 0870 609 3476
Web: www.support-dogs.org.uk